The Reality of the Spiritual World

One Man's Journey Into and Out of The Abyss

By

Nathan Pera, Sr.

authorHOUSE™

1663 LIBERTY DRIVE, SUITE 200
BLOOMINGTON, INDIANA 47403
(800) 839-8640
WWW.AUTHORHOUSE.COM

First published by AuthorHouse 11/01/04

ISBN: 1-4184-9583-2 (sc)

Printed in the United States of America
Bloomington, Indiana

This book is printed on acid-free paper.

ACKNOWLEDGEMENTS

I have been allowed to experience the reality of the spiritual world. By worldly standards this knowledge has been both terrifying and reassuring. It has brought me anxiety and tranquility, emotional highs and lows, and the unfolding of these experiences has tried my patience and sanity, and sometimes that of those closest to me.

My endless love and thanks to:

- My wife, Carroll Ann, who is always supportive and patient, no matter how bizarre things become.

- My children who also give me support in two distinctively different manners.

- My dearest and most spiritually influential friends Joel and Lee Jennings, whom we met as young couples in the Chicago area in the 1960s. Who would have thought that 25 years later that friendship would be resurrected and come to be so instrumental in my spiritual growth?

- My two small groups over the past 10 years that have taught me so much about the ever presence of the Holy Spirit, the meaning of the Body of Christ and the place to find counsel when trust and confidentiality are essential. That current group consists of my long time spiritual soul mates, Billy Vaughan, Al Holliday, Jack Acor, Bill Marler, Mike Touchet and Don Moore. Don has also has been my editor in this venture.

- James A. Meade, Msc.D. who opened the door to the metaphysical world for me on that day in May of 1993. I had been looking for that door for some 20 years. He still spends his time helping souls find their way.

- Richard G. Schulman, Ph.D. a clinical psychologist of 20 years who continues to work on the cutting edge of psychotherapy using a sophisticated approach to bio-feedback. Schulman Foundation for Trans-somatic Therapy.

I would also like to thank three people who have been influential in my putting these words to paper. The first is a retired Methodist minister, Berkley Poole, who for the past 20 years has spent his time as a spiritual director walking with many Christians and non-Christians on their journeys back to God. Berkley is a mystic, but prefers to be called an intuitive. To him and his wife Dot, and their youngest child Maggie, I am grateful for the comfort, guidance, friendship and delicious figs they serve with abundance in their north Mississippi retreat home.

The second is Dr. Mary McDonald, Superintendent of Schools for the Diocese of Memphis. Mary was the final straw that encouraged me to share my experiences, and therefore my writing with the world. Mutual encouragement, understanding and support would be the phrase that best describes our relationship. It was her rather objective encouragement to publish my stories that pushed me over the edge and gave me the impetus to pull this book together.

The third is my friend Reverend Sam Pace, another Methodist minister, who came to the cloth at the age of 40, and so brings to his ministry an earthiness that I easily relate to. Rev. Sam and I share much of the same philosophies and theology. He recently told me a story of a seminary professor who was discussing theology with his class. He asked the class if anyone could describe their theology. Hands went up, but the professor dismissed the presentations as being a rehash of recognized theologians who had already reduced their thoughts to writing. Finally, feigning frustration, the professor told his class to move on to another exercise. He asked them to take a half sheet of paper and write down something from their childhood that had a memorable affect on their lives. When the young seminarians had completed their task he told them, "Take your story home and reflect on it, and from your reflections develop the answers to the following questions;

Who is God?

What is good?

What is evil?

What is salvation?

What is sin?

What is forgiveness?

What is reconciliation?

When you have found the answers to those questions in your story, you will know your theology."

Sam was the first to encourage me to write my story. Perhaps, like the seminary professor, he set me up, knowing that if I wrote my story, if nothing else it would answer the questions that would unveil my theology to myself. I have said that if this writing helped just one person understand their relationship with God it would be worth the effort. It has already helped me.

TABLE OF CONTENTS

PART I

Nathan Pera, Sr.

CHAPTER 1
INTRODUCTION

My life has unfolded in 10-year cycles. As I reflect on those cycles I recall that some were stressful and slow, while others were fulfilling and moved like time did not exist. I have come to realize that the slow years were periods of learning. They were hard times that tested my endurance and commitment to my chosen path, or in some cases, a path yet to be known. The fast years were the fulfillment of my purpose. Things moved smoothly, with seemingly little or no effort on my part. As I begin to write about these experiences in my life I am coming out of my sixth life cycle. This one has been hard and slow. This time I am better prepared than I was for my cycles as a younger man. Experience is a great equalizer. It gives one the advantage of having lived through the ups and downs of life. Like a picture is worth a thousand words, memories of experiences offer myriad pictures of a lifetime.

If you choose to read this book, you will read true stories of how one man sees himself making his way retrospectively through the awakening of the unknown side of his life and then, in later years, in the presence of the Now. While my memory is clear back to my third year of life, I can only be aware of an unseen force in my life since the age of 17 years and 11 months, when

I met my soul mate and instantly recognized she would be my wife.

I have divided the book in to two Parts. Part I describes my initial, unexpected interaction with the paranormal; the struggles with holding on to my sanity and those who were there to support me. Part II is a compilation of stories that describe the lessons I learned as I continually sought to know more about the God who had revealed himself to me through my physical senses.

These are stories that took me through unsolicited and bizarre experiences into the unknown. To date I have no clear vision of why I was granted what I have come to call "My Blessings." I am a Christian who has experienced the reality of the spiritual world. There is a difference between being spiritual and experiencing a Christian salvation. The sequence of stories will reflect the spiritual evolution from shedding spiritual attachments, to the acceptance of Jesus Christ as my Lord and Savior, to receiving daily gifts of spiritual intervention.

Some will say it is fiction. Some will say it was Satan. I hope that this writing will reveal that God works in mysterious ways with all of His created souls. Christian churches have historically discouraged their members from pursuing unsupervised contact with the spiritual world, and I have come to understand their position. For there is no way to be sure if the contact is of God, or of Satan, until one is fairly well down the road. My intention was to tether myself to God and make it perfectly clear that I was only interested in seeking a contact with Him. In Matthew (12:25-26) Jesus says, "A house divided cannot stand." So the questions I used for evaluation have been: Has real and true good come from my experiences? Is there Biblical support for the experiences being of God? Is there any violation of God's basic moral laws?

Some may say I have misinterpreted the Bible. In the 1500s the church accused Martin Luther of heresy for changes that have become known as the Protestant Reformation. Psychologists may deem these stories as illusionary and having no basis of reality. I am not selling my theology, nor am I concerned with proving my sanity. These are simply true stories I have experienced in the company of my loving wife and soul mate, Carroll Ann, who always has been there to steady me when I felt that I might be losing my mind, or that I was about to fall into the abyss.

Each of us journeys through our earthly life alone. We may find a loving soul mate whom we know is our stabilizing partner. We may have close friends from whom we can seek counsel in our sometimes lengthy periods of need. We may or may not belong to an organized church that offers spiritual and practical fellowship. Yet with all of these crutches we come to understand that we make this trip into, and ultimately out of, this world alone. Or do we?

CHAPTER 2
THE BACKGROUND

M y true spiritual awakening began on May 28, 1993 in a most unexpected and bizarre way. It is the subject of this book, but before I tell the story, as my long time Canadian friend often says, "you need some background."

I was the oldest of four siblings born to Nathan and Prudentia Pera. When I was seven years old, and living in a nice middle class neighborhood, I was sexually seduced by a young male teenage neighbor. I use the word "seduced" rather than "abused" because even today at age 62 I cannot come to refer to the encounter as abusive. In the middle 1990s there was a rash of "child abuse" cases splayed across the newspapers and on television. I remember watching and observing that the experts, as well as parents, were confounded by the happenings. Everyone seemed perplexed by the silence of the children. It came as no surprise to me. Even to a seven-year-old, who did not reach puberty until my sophomore year in high school, the sexual encounters were pleasurable. If physical pain is not part of the experience then it is not difficult to understand that most children would not come forward voluntarily. It may come as a surprise to adults who never experienced sexual pleasure as children, but significant sexual pleasure can be experienced by a seven-year-old. Perhaps a lack of personal experience of this pleasure on the part of the investigating adults was the reason the entire episode was perplexing and a mystery to them.

There can be long lasting psychological damage incurred by the youngster who is seduced. Most often the encounter is terminated as the older person tires of it, finds a new outlet, becomes afraid of getting caught, or as in my case, is discovered by observant parents. In the 1940s there was little or no awareness of child psychology, so like my crooked teeth, my life would not get straightened out until I was confronted with the festering problems many years later.

At age 24 I was married to my high school sweetheart Carroll Ann and our first child, a boy we named Nathan IV, was born 10 months later. At age 26 I became innocently and yet insidiously, addicted to pornography. I was a young man in his prime. It started innocently enough. I would come home at night from a long day at work and have dinner with my wife and young son. My wife would put our baby to bed, while I worked on projects around the house. The last thing I did every night was to light up my one cigarette for the day and go into the bathroom for my daily constitutional and 15 minutes of total solitude. It was the one place and time of the day that was totally mine. It seemed only right that I should have the privilege of losing my self in the monthly issue of *Playboy,* and later *Penthouse*, for that brief fantasy escape. It seemed innocent enough, and though my wife complained about me reading "that garbage," I insisted "It meant nothing to me and it did no harm"- words I would many years later regret, and learn were not true.

As time went by, the pornography deepened. Viewing stag films was common among young men. I became interested in viewing and reading about homosexual encounters. Though I was not seriously attracted to sex with men, watching or reading about it intrigued me. No doubt this interest stemmed from my encounter with the teenage male as a child.

Three years after our son was born and about 18 months after my pornographic addiction began, we had our second child, a beautiful baby girl we named Theresa. Unlike our son, who was outgoing and demanding of our constant attention, Theresa was quiet and would play by herself in her playpen for long periods of time. To us she was a Godsend. As you will come to understand later in this writing we came to realize that in this quiet time Theresa had been playing with her "friends."

I was hesitant to allow myself to get close to my daughter. I had read that persons who have sexual experiences as children often become the aggressor with their own children. Fortunately for us, and by the grace of God, that was not true in our case. However, there would be other problems in our relationship, many originating from the little-remembered encounter some 20 years earlier. It was between the births of Nathan and Theresa that one evening during a telephone conversation my mother related to me that my young seducer had been killed in an automobile accident at the age of 31. It was a passing statement that meant little to me at the time.

In 1983, at the age of 45, I had my first awareness that God was trying to communicate with me. I was financially successful and had owned my own business for 11 years. I had the feeling that I was supposed to be doing something, giving something back, but I could not put my finger on it. Then one day at Sunday mass I heard our pastor give a homily that said "we are called by God to feed the hungry and clothe the naked." I knew at that moment that God was calling me to feed the poor. It turned out not to be as simple as it sounds, but that episode led me to contemplate who, and where, God was. I concluded that He was a real being, resided in a different dimension, where time was not a factor, and He could be everywhere at once. I also knew that while He was good to me, man was not the end of the food chain, and I was subservient to Him/Her. This hip pocket theology of mine, developed between 1975 and 1992, would play a much bigger part in my life than I could have ever imagined.

In January 1990, when I was 50 years old, came the most traumatic occurrence of my life, when my mother, to whom I was extremely close emotionally, was diagnosed with stomach cancer. At the time it was not obvious, but I took ill at essentially the same time. My illness started in November 1989. By mid-January 1990 I became incapacitated. I was constantly nauseated and couldn't eat. I lost 20 pounds in about two months. I became weak, with no energy. I suffered the most horrendous emotional pain one could imagine. I knew before anyone else in the family that she would undergo successful surgery, but a reoccurrence within six months would inevitably take her life. Perhaps she knew too. For 18 months I could think of nothing else. Later I would reflect that this episode in my life, though so painful that I explained with the statement, "I couldn't be feeling this bad unless I was dying," prolonged my life on this earth. The pain drove me to seek the help of a psychologist who introduced me to a young man who was trained in relaxation methods. The relaxation techniques made the final stages of my mother's illness more bearable, and have led me to be receptive to a better understanding of the power of the human mind and its effect on the body.

In my adult life from age 35 to 50, I believed I was in complete control. Not that I didn't recognize that God was very much a part of my success, but just that I was accustomed to "making things happen" the way we needed them to be. With my mother's illness I was finally confronted with a problem that I could not fix, and all the money I had couldn't buy an acceptable resolution. In her final stages, one day I told her I would give up everything I had if I could take her illness from her. Many difficult lessons can be faced by family members, as well as non-family members, at the deathbeds of loved ones and strangers alike.

God often allows us to descend to the depths of our own living hell and brokenness before He throws us the lifeline we so desperately need but cannot recognize until we have no other choice. Such was my case when, after several years of struggling and suffering, God put into motion a sequence of events that would lead me to shed my albatrosses, one by one, and be slowly and methodically led to experience the physical manifestation of God's presence and glory with my worldly senses. A person who has experienced God with one or more of the physical senses will never be the same again. It is not for anyone to say why some are blessed with these manifestations and some are not, except to say that God recognizes what we need before we know it and He gives to those who are in need. It has been a long and often turbulent journey for me, and yet as every day passes I find more and more comfort in the knowledge of the real presence of God within me. For instance, He has edited this writing as it progressed, in a simple little way that He and I share.

CHAPTER 3
THE AWAKENING

The stage was set in 1988. Though I loved my work, I began having the feeling that I should pull away from my business. I felt God was calling me, but for what? So I halfheartedly tried to turn the business over to my two key and long-time managers. Nothing worked and so, by the beginning of 1990, I was no further along than I had been in 1988. Finally God laid me on my back. As discussed earlier, my illness coincided with my mother's diagnosis of terminal cancer. However, my symptoms started prior to her diagnosis, so I have been hesitant to believe that my illness was directly due to hers. In hindsight, I would certainly accept the fact that God allowed the two to come together in such a fashion as to maximize my reaction.

I was light headed and nauseous all day every day. My one relief, which points to mental depression, was that the nausea left when I lay down and, fortunately, I could sleep. I visited countless doctors of all sorts, including those at Mayo Clinic in Rochester, Minnesota. No physiological reason for my illness could be detected. Then I truly did become depressed. Doctors would say, "You're depressed. Take these antidepressants." My reaction was "if you felt as bad as I do and could not

get any relief or reason for it, you'd be depressed too."
I refused to take the pills. They made me feel jittery.

My life as I had known it, a good 16 hours a day of work or project activity, was over. I could function only about three or four hours per day and the rest of the time I spent in my recliner, recovering from that brief amount of physical activity. Finally one day I went to a minor emergency clinic and a young doctor asked me if anybody had investigated my ears as the possible source of the problem. I said no. He gave me a prescription for an over-the-counter antihistamine called Antivert. One day of those pills and the symptoms were gone. Yet no ear specialist could detect any source for the problem. Later I learned that common earplugs accomplished the same results. Obviously I had overly sensitive ear canals that, when stressed, led to an imbalance that brought on the symptoms. To this day an overdose of stress brings on the same reaction. Through inner work described in later chapters and other writings, I have learned to recognize and release most stressful encounters.

Time moves on, and by age 50 I was a successful owner of two businesses. We were making money and our children were healthy, at least physically. By this time I was deep into the pornography and it was getting heavier and heavier. By now it was so bad that I kept it locked in a toolbox in our bedroom closet. Now the time for reading or viewing was not limited to the 15 minutes at the end of my day. It often became part of my lunchtime break. I was near the bottom, spiritually and morally speaking. Later I would reflect on this time and realize that I was on the verge of losing my marriage, my family and probably my businesses and either didn't realize it, or really care. My wife and I had drifted further apart, as she abhorred the material and could sense the evil that was raging in my soul.

As 1992 began I was engulfed by three prevalent illnesses - Chronic Fatigue Syndrome (CFS), a violent physical reaction to any type of wheat or grain-based food or alcohol, and the emotional pain caused by my mother's terminal illness. When my mother died in April of 1990 the latter pain instantly evaporated, making me feel significantly better. Yet I still suffered from lack of energy and the food sensitivities.

I began working on the fatigue problem myself. I researched books on CFS and found that a book entitled *Chronic Fatigue Syndrome* by Drs. Stoff and Pellegrino helped improve my immune system. A monthly publication, *Prevention,* led me to discover the natural herbal extract *Echinacea Agustifolia* that gave me an almost instant increase in energy.

It was two months after the passing of my mother that my sister Mary encouraged me to visit a hypnotherapist she had met at a friend's home, to help me with my stomach problem. My reaction was "people get hypnotized to stop smoking and to lose weight, so why not try it." So the stage was set.

On May 28, 1993 I walked into a holistic medicine clinic in Memphis, and met Jim Meade. Jim was a stout man of medium height with a deep, raspy, but warm and pleasant voice. We exchanged pleasantries and briefly discussed why I was there, which was, in my mind, to have him hypnotize the food allergies away. Being a very cautious and controlling person, I had brought along my sister, wife, and daughter to witness the episode. I was not inclined to let a stranger mess with my mind without some dependable allies to look out for my best interest.

Jim asked me some questions about my general physical and mental conditions and attitudes, which I answered in much the manner I have described above. With the preliminaries behind us he suggested we get started. It was about 4 p.m. when Jim started the hypnosis process.

Many people have various misconceptions of what hypnosis is and/or feels like. I would liken it to any of the following:

* Driving down the highway by yourself and suddenly wondering where you have been for the past 10 minutes, yet knowing that you were conscious enough to drive and make decisions.

* Following a daydream to the extent you lose contact with those around you and are jolted out of that feeling by the irritating question "where have you been?"

* Talking on a cell phone while driving and then hanging up and not remember driving from A to B, yet knowing that all along you were conscious of what was happening around you.

In other words, a person under hypnosis is present and knows what is happening and yet allows the subconscious to surface and be heard. It is much like meditation with a facilitator.

Transcript from MAY 28, 1993

I took to Jim immediately. That feeling would grow into friendship, one that continues to this day. The room was rather large and there were comfortable floor cushions around the room. Jim asked that my family recline on them and remain quiet unless he asked for their assistance. I sat in a large recliner and Jim began the process. After the hypnotic induction was completed, Jim continued to speak in a very melodic and deep voice.

(Jim:) *"Okay let us begin, Nathan. Subconscious mind. Subconscious mind, I want you to feel the joy, the peace and happiness associated with the word yes. In a few moments I am going to ask you to make one of Nathan's fingers move indicating the word yes. Nathan, you may or may not be aware that the fingers are moving or attempting to move. I do not want you to concern yourself with this. I want you to allow your conscious mind to go to a different time, to a different place. It may even be a fantasy of its own choice. To remain there until I call it back.*

And once again subconscious I want you to feel the joy, the peace and happiness associated with the word yes. And I now want you to cause one of his fingers to move indicating to me the word yes, and to do that now." (Long pause.)

Jim in a very deep, slow and rhythmical tone:

"Deeper. . ., and deeper. Down . ., down . ., down. Each and every breath, subconscious, carries him deeper . . as he steps aside . ., .steps aside. Subconscious, I am going to gently touch him on the arm. The energies that I send you subconscious are going to give you more control over the fingers. Use the energies. You are in control of the hands and fingers, subconscious."

Jim continues,

"I now want you to cause one finger to move and to move strongly, indicating to me the word yes, and to do that now."

17

(Pause, then the right index finger lifts.)

"I understand. You may relax the finger. You may relax that finger. Subconscious, I now want you to chose a different finger to move indicating to me the word no, and to do that now."

(Pause, then the right little finger lifts.)

"I understand, you may relax that finger."

"Subconscious I am going to release the arm but the energy is going to continue to flow to you. It's going to flow. The more and more you move the fingers, the more and more Nathan steps aside . . .. Steps aside."

Jim asks the question:

"Subconscious mind, you are the one who guides and protects him?"

(Pause, then the yes finger raises.)

"Yes, I understand. And subconscious mind you are the one who has recorded every experience, in his present lifetime or any previous lifetimes, is this also true?"

(Pause, then the yes finger rises.)

"Yes. Alright subconscious, you may relax that finger."

"Subconscious mind, Nathan has come to me today. He is asking for my assistance in helping him. But I need your assistance subconscious for you know him much better than I. Are you willing to help me with this?"

(The yes finger rises.)

"Yes. Thank you subconscious."

"Subconscious mind I want you to check Nathan's memory banks. I want you to check. Is there something going on in the present lifetime that is causing the stomach problems, and the other things that we have discussed?"

(Long pause, then the yes finger rises. Jim repeats the question.)

"Yes. Subconscious mind I am going to touch him on the arm again. You are in control of the fingers." Pause. *"Is there something going on in the present lifetime?"*

(The yes finger rises again.)

"Yes, there is, I understand, you may relax that finger."

"Subconscious mind, does it have anything to do with the aura that surrounds him?"

(The yes finger rises.)

"Yes, it does. I understand. I want you to examine his aura. I want you to examine his aura from head to toe, front to back, and side to side. When you have thoroughly and completely examined his aura I want you to signal me with the yes finger, and to do that now."

(Long pause, then the yes finger rises.)

"All right subconscious, you have completely and thoroughly examined the aura. Now subconscious mind, in the light of truth and in the light of knowledge, are there spirits in, or attached, to his aura?"

(Pause, then the yes finger rises.)

"I am going to touch him on the arm. There is no outside interference. There can be no outside interference, subconscious. You are the one who guides and protects him. I ask you again, are there spirits within his aura?"

(Pause, the no finger rises.)

"I want you to examine it again subconscious. In the light of truth and knowledge."

(There is a long pause.)

"Is there someone within the aura?"

(The yes finger rises again. Then suddenly I begin to omit audible sighs and groans, preceded by slight sobbing. Jim continues talking in a compassionate voice.)

"Mother is there, isn't she? She came to Nathan when she made the transition. You didn't go on, did you dear?"

(There is an increase in my audible sobbing.)

"You didn't go on did you dear?"

(A series of audible and apparently painful "Ahgs" originate from my throat as I feel my back arching off the chair.)

(Jim speaks authoritatively.)

"And now you are going to have to leave him, and he is going to have to let go of you."

(I am now sobbing. Jim continues to speak.)

"I want you to look at each other."

(I am audibly sobbing and crying.)

"That's right You have known each other before, you know that."

(I am crying uncontrollably.)

"Isn't that right my dear? Yes. I knew it when we started. I knew you were there."

(I am crying intensely now.)

"But I send you peace and love."

(Louder sobbing and crying at this point.)

"Let it go Nathan, its all right. Let it out."

(Continued loud crying.)

"Let it out. I know it hurts. You knew each other before. I know that. But now the two of you have got to let go of each other."

(Jim continues as my sobbing is reduced.)

"Is there anyone here she wants to say anything to before she goes?"

(My yes finger rises.)

"You can speak through Nathan. I know you are sorry that you came. That's why he felt the change so quickly after your passing. Isn't that true?"

(I am sobbing.)

"Yes that's right. That is why he felt the change so quickly. For 18 months you were in torment and the moment she died it was like it was okay, because she then came to you. That's right, she penetrated your aura. She came to your light."

(Jim Meade speaks again.)

"Prudy, I know you can hear me. I send you love my dear."

(Mama speaks in pain through my voice.)

"Yes, yes, God, it hurts so bad."

"She knew she had to be here today." (I speak for myself while sobbing and talking incoherently about why Mama and I were there.)

(Jim continues to speak to Mama.)

"We all love you. You were loved when you were here. Yes, but now its time to go on. It's time for you to leave. You must go and prepare the way for your husband."

(Mama, speaks through my voice.)

"My husband, my husband, my husband," (Her voice trails off). *No, my daughter is here for my husband. My daughter is here for my husband."*

(I am sobbing again uncontrollably.)

Jim: *"Do you want to talk to your daughter Prudy? Umh?"*

(I sob as Jim continues.)

"Mary is going to touch Nathan's other hand Prudy."

"Its cold. My hand is ice cold." (I Sob and moan, ugghh, in anguish.)

(Mama speaks through my voice again.)

"You took care of me. You took care of me.

Jim: *"Who took care of you?"*

24

(Mama speaks through my voice again.)

"My daughter, Mary, she took care of me while I was dying. I didn't die fast enough. I made them suffer, I made them all suffer."

(Jim continues to talk to Mama.)

"Do you feel guilty about making them suffer?"

Mama: *"Yes I guess . . . . "*

Jim: *"No, no. Do not feel guilty. They loved you."*

Mama: *"Yes."*

(Jim, in an assuring voice to Mama.)

"It was their choice to take care of you, as it was your choice to die. God did not call you home. You chose to die."

Mama: *"I don't understand."*

Jim: *"I will bring some understanding to you. I'm going to touch him on the shoulder. My brothers I want you to bring the light down around Nathan. I ask my brothers from the brotherhood of white light to bring her records to her. Bring her book of life to her. You have been on this earth plane many times my dear. Let my brothers explain to you now what I am saying."*

(There is quiet in the room. As I reflect on the tape I have the feeling that my mother's spirit is being made aware of her book of life and that Jim is also aware of what is being transmitted.)

"Do you understand Prudy?"

(Mama starts to speak through my voice.)

"I don't know, I can only say what I think."

(Jim apparently completes Mama's thought telepathically, as he continues.)

"Yes, you are going to be back again."

Mama: *"That's what I hear."*

Jim: *"That's right, you will be back again."*

(Jim continues to speak.)

"But Nathan is going to help prepare a new place on this earth, along with everybody else who is here. Make it a new and better place for everybody. No wars, no more hurt, pain and anger. Wouldn't you like that?"

Mama: *"Yes."*

Jim: *"But you need to help from the spirit side. You need to clear his aura today. Is there anyone else there with you?"*

(I sigh and there is a long pause.)

Jim: *"Do you feel the sense of anyone else there with you in his aura?"*

Mama: *"I don't know."*

Jim: *"That's okay, it's all right. If there is anyone else there I will help them leave too."*

(Jim speaks to Mama.)

"Are you ready to go with my brothers? Do you see the beautiful light? Look yes, yes. Prudy! Look into the light."

Mama: *"I have seen it before."*

Jim: *"My brothers I want you to bring Prudy's mother to her. She has been looking for her. Do you see her? Do you feel her presence with you? It is time to go. It is time to leave Nathan now, forever. But forever is not forever. You have been together before and that is why you felt so close to him."*

(I am crying again.)

Jim*: "Do not be frightened. It is a beautiful place over there. You don't want Nathan to be hurting anymore do you? No, you don't want him to be hurting. Are you ready to go?"*

(I sigh.)

Jim: *"Nathan, are you ready to let her go?"*

(I respond hesitantly.)

"I thought I did a long time ago."

Jim: *"No she came to you. Are you ready to let her go now?"*

(Again, I speak hesitantly.)

"I would hope so. I think so."

Jim. *"I want you to be sure. It has got to be done."*

(I respond in a more assured voice.)

"There is nothing to be gained by her staying here."

Jim *"Yes, there is nothing to be gained by her staying here. She is locked up like a genie in a bottle. You wouldn't want that."*

Jim: *"All right, don't be frightened Prudy. My brothers, bring down the light. Guide her home. These two release each other now. In Christ's light. Say goodbye to Nathan. You only gave him birth this time, but he chose you. Say goodbye to him. Say goodbye to her, Nathan."*

(I am sobbing and crying.)

Jim continues: *"Say goodbye to her, Nathan. Yes, the genie is coming out of the bottle. She gets to go and fly among the stars."*

(I am now crying.)

Jim continues: *"Number one, feeling her being lifted out. Take her my brothers gently. We send her in love. Number two, going into the light. And number three, going, going, going, gone. Let her go. Watch her disappear Nathan, watch her disappear. Feel the peace that she has left you. Feel the love that fills you now. There is no void. There is no greater gift from a mother to her son than to free him."*

(I sigh.)

Jim: *"Subconscious, may I bring him back to full awareness?"*

(My yes finger rises.)

"He has been through much right now. All right, all right, Nathan. She is gone. I want you to feel the sense of peace and tranquility. It's okay."

"Number one coming up. You are now at peace inside. You are at peace with her. She is flying among the stars. Number two coming up even more. Feeling a sense of joy and happiness. Feel the love she left behind for you. She is gone. Number three coming up even more. Number four coming up even more, and number five eyes open and back with me."

(When I came out of the hypnotic trance I spoke about what had transpired to Jim and my family, who had witnessed this mind-boggling experience. I looked around at Jim and my family and spoke excitedly.)

"I know everything that happened. I haven't been gone, but you would know that."

Jim: *"That's right you are aware of everything that happened."*

(I continue excitedly.)

"I know I spoke in my mother's voice. Not my mother's voice but I spoke as her. And I did not feel hypnotized. I never felt like I left."

(Calmly Jim asks me.)

"But what does it feel like to be hypnotized?"

(I exclaim still in disbelief myself.)

"I'm just telling you that I was aware of what was going on at all times. I wasn't off in la-la land. I never felt gone."

Jim: *"But you know when I started pushing buttons something happened."*

"Yes," (I nod.)

"My fingers did rise on their own. Until you touched me they didn't. At first I wanted to make them rise and I wanted them to rise because I said to myself 'I'm not hypnotized, but I'll do it anyway.' But I didn't. Then you touched me on the arm and it happened."

(I continue.)

"My hands are ice cold."

"I remember when you said my mother was with me, and the physical feelings I had, and the manifestation and I knew that the voice became a different gender than myself. How could I have been so conscious if I were hypnotized?"

Jim: *"You did a great job, Nathan."*

(I am crying again.)

Jim: *"Go ahead, its all right to cry."*

(I sob more intensely.)

Jim: *It's okay, just let it go. Let the emotions out."*

(I cry and sob as I become more aware of those around me.)

"Carroll Ann, are you all right? Theresa are you all right?"

(I ask Jim.)

"Why would I have this fatigue thing?"

Jim: *"I don't know. Right now you are on an emotional cliff. That is why I brought you back up."*

(I sigh in resignation.)

"Yes, I guess I am."

Jim: *"It's all right and it is okay to be there. It's good to let those emotions out. You've got to discharge them. That is what is causing a lot of your disorders. You have been hanging onto all these emotions."*

(I agree.)

Jim: *"I'm not sure what is causing the fatigue. I believe we have more work to do."*

(I question Jim.)

"How I am I supposed to feel about my mother now?"

Jim: *"You are going to have a feeling of love. Just the love she left behind."*

(I ask, fearful of his answer.)

"Should I be afraid that thinking of her is going to bring her back?"

Jim: *"The only way she can penetrate your aura again is if she wants back and you agree to let her back. It must be a mutual agreement at this point. She came to you in love when she died, possibly to say goodbye. In some cases loved ones sense a need for protection in one being left behind, and that is the reason they stay."*

(His comment stirs me to recall a recent event.)

"Me and my sister had a talk about Mama's death when she died. My sister said that when Mama died I told her to let go, that God was waiting for her. Yesterday, when I related this to my wife I started crying for no obvious reason."

Jim: *"That is because your mother knew the truth. She was in your aura. She was there and you were feeling her. That is why you cried. She was saying, 'No Nathan I didn't go. I'm here with you.' But this has been resolved."*

(I speak, shaking my head in disbelief.)

"I can't believe this is actually happening to me."

Jim: *"Nathan, I think we need to continue looking at your aura. Are you up to it today?"*

(I respond affirmatively, fearful of what else might be uncovered.)

"Yes, I couldn't leave here without knowing what else might be going on."

(At this point Jim went through the hypnotic induction again and the agreement with my subconscious to answer questions concerning my aura. We continue the transcript below.)

Jim: *"Subconscious. I want you to examine his aura again. I want you to examine his aura from head to toe, front to back, and side-to-side. When you have thoroughly and completely examined his aura I want you to signal me with the yes finger, and to do that now."*

(There is a long pause, and Jim continues.)

"All right. Subconscious, you have completely and thoroughly examined the aura. Now subconscious mind, in the light of truth and in the light of knowledge, are there spirits in his aura?"

(Pause and the yes finger rises.)

Jim: *"I am going to touch him on the arm. There is no outside interference. There can be no outside interference, subconscious. You are the one who guides and protects him. I ask you again, are there spirits within his aura?"*

(Pause and the yes finger rises.)

Jim: *"Subconscious is there more than one entity in his aura?"*

(Pause and the yes finger rises.)

Jim: *"Yes, I understand. Subconscious, are there more than two entities in his aura?"*

(Another pause and the yes finger rises.)

Jim: *"Yes subconscious. I understand. Subconscious, are there more than three entities in his aura?"*

(There is a longer pause and the no finger rises.)

Jim: *"Yes subconscious I understand. You may relax that finger now. Subconscious are there three entities in his aura?"*

(There is a pause and the yes finger rises.)

Jim: *"Yes subconscious. I understand there are three entities in his aura."*

(Jim continues to inquire.)

"Subconscious are the entities within Nathan's aura deceased relatives of his?"

(There is a pause and the yes finger rises.)

"Yes, I under. . ." (As Jim starts to continue my no finger also raises. Jim observes the discrepancy.)

Jim: *"Subconscious you have indicated a yes and a no. Is this correct?"*

(The yes finger rises.)

Jim: *"Subconscious are there both relatives and non-relatives in his aura?"*

(My yes finger rises.)

"Are there two relatives and one non-relative?"

(Pause and my yes finger rises.)

Jim: *"I understand subconscious. You may relax that finger now."*

"Subconscious let us first deal with the relatives. Is the grandmother there?"

(My yes finger rises.)

Jim: *"I understand."*

"Is the grandfather also there?"

(My yes finger rises.)

Jim: *"Subconscious, does either one of them want to talk to anyone here before they leave Nathan's aura?"*

(I am breathing rather normally at this time and there is no audible sign of emotion in my breathing or voice. At this point I begin to speak.)

"They seem to be arguing. I can't understand what is being said. I believe they are speaking in Italian."

Jim: *"That is all right. That is all right. Does either of them want to speak?"*

(I respond.)

"Yes, my grandmother says she has a message for my father."

Jim: *"Okay. That is okay. You may speak to us grandmother. You may use Nathan's voice to give us your message."*

(Grandmother speaks, using my voice.)

"Tell Nathan, my son, that I loved him, but I could not show him my love because his two brothers took everything I had."

Jim: *"We understand your message and it will be delivered to your son after you have left."*

(At this point my breathing is becoming heavy and labored. Suddenly I moan audibly.)

"God I have the ability to draw thingggs to meeeee. Spirits, to meee". (Sigh. . .sigh), *"and that scares me. Ahgh."* (I moan in fright.)

(Jim assumes control of the situation.)

"I want all of you in Nathan's aura to listen to me now. This one is getting very tired."

(I repeat his words in an exhausted whisper.)

"Very tired."

(Jim speaks authoritatively to the three spirits in my aura.)

"My brothers are going to be with all of you. The light is going to be with Nathan and they are going to follow him. They are going to follow all of you. When Nathan's father receives the message from his mother and understands what is going on. (I am whimpering.) *You will then leave within three days. Do you understand?"*

(I interject audibly.)

"They do."

Jim: *"It is very important that you understand. Either you will leave on your own or my brothers will come and take you. But they don't want to do that. But I will charge them with those orders. This aura will be cleared, completely. Do all of you understand this?"*

(I respond in a barely audible whisper.)

"My grandmother understands."

(I am whimpering in exhaustion, sobbing and crying.)

Jim, *"All right. I do not wish this one to get any worse. He is very tired and exhausted."*

"My brothers, I am going to place a mark on his forehead. The mark of the Brotherhood of White Light. I charge you now with his protection. I want the light

40

to follow him. So be it now. You are charged with him and with the ones in his aura. This is to be resolved very soon."

(I continue whimpering at the realization of what is going on.)

"All right." (Says Jim.) *"I am going to bring him back to full awareness. This story must be told, and that is okay."*

Jim: *"Number one. Coming up. Number two, Coming up even* more."

(I am sighing and sobbing, crying in emotional pain.)

"Number three coming up even more, number four you are much more aware of my voice, and number five eyes open and you are back with me."

(As I come out of the hypnotic trance I begin sobbing and crying in release of the stress. I sob hysterically.)

"I know everything that happened and what was said. God!!!!! I can bring these spirits into myself. Why me?"

(I repeat.)

"Why me? Because I'm receptive. That's why."
(Answering my own question.)

(Jim asks me the question.)

"Are you asking why is this happening to you? You are the intermediary between all of them. You are the one who ties it all together."

(Frightened I ask.)

"Am I capable of bringing more of these entities into my aura?"

Jim: *"I would say you didn't consciously draw them, I think when your grandmother passed over you were the link between her and her son, your father." I don't know what the sequence of events of who all are here. Your grandmother passed away last. We know your grandfather is there, but we still don't know who the third spirit in your aura is, or why that entity is there."*

At this point, without provocation and in a conscious state, I revealed my first messages from a source that was unknown to me at that time. It was only in transcribing this tape that I realized the following had transpired, although it occurred many times in later encounters with those in psychological need.

"Now I hear." (This is the only preface to the following statements to those in the room with me.)

"Now I hear that Mary has to know that my father is going to be in the same situation. He can't leave this earth by himself."

(I continue the messages, addressing my daughter.)

"And then Theresa needs to know that she will not leave here. . . I don't mean to scare her, but until you (Theresa) deal with your mother and me at a different level you will be in that same position. Your spirit will be held here by one of us, or by yourself. Okay? Do you understand?"

(Theresa asks.)

"You mean when I die?"

(I reply to her.)

Yes, that's right."

(I return my attention to my sister.)

"Mary, this is important for you because you will be where our father will stay. That's why I said what I said."

(My sister asks.)

"You mean I will take his spirit when he dies?"

(I reply.) *"Yes, unless you help him along at his passing. Be aware."*

(I returned to Theresa and speak.)

"You are in the same position that my father was in with his mother. Ohhh."

This ended the messages to those in the room.

Jim regains control: *"You are tired Nathan. We need to let you rest. You've been through a lot. How are you feeling now, drained? Yea?"*

(Jim then summarizes what has happened and what is to happen.)

"Understand the sequence of events coming up from the spirit side. Okay? You have been placed in the hands of the ones I work with, The Brotherhood of White Light. Once this sequence of events takes place and your father knows what he needs to know and so on, the spirits will have to leave your aura within three days, even if they have to be taken out. Even if they have to be extracted they will be removed from your aura. They do not have the right to be there anymore.

They have had their say. We now know the sequence of events. All you have to do is deliver the message to your father then you will be free. My feeling is that this will help develop a bond or understanding between you and your father. Ultimately the grandmother wants to talk to her son through you. So you must deliver the message."

(Shaking my head in the negative, I reply.)

"But my father will never believe this. He is not a believer of the spiritual world."

(Jim replies.)

"Beliefs don't count, it does not matter. She has the right to say her piece through you. Once she says her piece, that's it. It is like Jesus when he walked into a town. They did not listen to what He had to say, he walked out, shook his sandals and walked on."

"The three spirits are still there. I have made an agreement with them that once the message has been delivered, they will be leaving. Whether they go willingly within the three days, or whether they are forced out. That is why you are under the charge of The Brotherhood of White Light."

(I ask.)

45

"You mean it will just happen?"

(Jim speaks with an audible crack in his voice.)

"Yes, once your father has received the message from his mother they will be gone within three days, one way or the other. When it happens. When it is all said and done and the final events take place, you will receive a sign so powerful, you will know. There will be no question in your mind. It will be an outward sign that will leave no doubt it has been done."

(I ask Jim.)

"What's wrong?"

Jim: *"Nothing, Nothing, it will be a beautiful moment for you."*

The session ended at approximately 6 p.m. In two short hours my world had been shockingly invaded. Through all the years of theorizing about the reality of the spiritual world, I was ill prepared for the sudden experience of its reality. Little did I know the first act of a long drama was scarcely underway.

NOTE; On Saturday, July 14, 2001 I completed another editing session of this chapter and I am full of doubts. I open my *Daily Catholic Devotional* and I read the thought for the day.

"Even though you meant harm to me, God meant it for good, to achieve his present end, the survival of many people." (Genesis 50:20)

"Can God bring good out of evil? It's a question for all ages. The story of Joseph and his brothers is one of the most moving tales of forgiveness in the scriptures. It is easy to see the good that came from the heartless ordeal of being sold into slavery in this story. But look a little closer to home. Are there memories of God drawing good out of evil in your life?

A woman once shared with me what she called "the story of her awakening." Only after her daughter ran away from home was she able to see how unjustly she had nagged and ridiculed the child. She also became aware that much of her harsh treatment was triggered by the jealousy she felt because of her daughter's youth and beauty. This great wound in her family led this mother to seek out counseling and renew her own life."

"Oh God of Forgiveness, make my heart vulnerable that I may be open to the revelation that waits for me on the other side of my sinfulness. Lift blessings out of my flawed life."
Sr. Macrina Wiederkehr, O.S. B.

As I re-read this chapter I am reminded that eight years later I am still free of the pornography addiction and all of the insidious thought patterns that came with it. I am not struggling with temptation on a daily basis, or living a life of abstinence requiring a support group, though I constantly seek spiritual camaraderie. The truth is, by the power and grace of God, the desire to read pornographic material has simply been removed. It brings to mind a question. What is the definition of a miracle? I believe that God was always with me and still is.

CHAPTER 4
THE EXORCISM AND
THE DREAM

Following my session with Jim my wife drove us home. I felt like a dishrag. As we walked into our entrance hall I had a sudden wave of terror come over me. The reality of what had just happened was taking hold. I stood at the bottom of the stairs and told Carroll Ann, "I can't stay here tonight. We need to go to a motel." Without any resistance she called and made us reservations at a local hotel. I fell asleep before my head hit the pillow.

As I recall my feelings, it was perhaps like a woman who had been raped would feel. I can only describe it as feeling like I had been violated, which of course, I had been in a spiritual sense. It was bad enough that my mother, grandmother and grandfather had spiritually been with me, but there was a fourth entity that was yet unknown. At this point my mind went wild trying to determine who, or what that entity could be and what was it doing in my spiritual space?

This was the first time I had felt like I was about to lose it, a feeling I would experience almost continually for the next few weeks. I couldn't decide whether this was

49

all a hallucination or reality. My daughter had said, as we left the clinic. "I would never have believed this if I hadn't heard and seen it with my own eyes."

Late the next morning we returned home. I now had been into my spiritual experience for 12 hours. I called my sister and told her that I had to deliver the message to our father that evening. She agreed and told me he would be at their home for supper. My wife and I arrived at her home shortly after the family had finished eating.

The room was thick with tension. Delivering a message like this from his deceased mother was hard to visualize. How would he react? Would he get angry and stomp out of the house telling us we were all crazy? I knew the clock was not running until I delivered the message to my father. It had been 24 hours since my session with Jim Meade and he had said that within three days of delivering the message to my father, the entities would either leave peacefully or be taken from me. Not until the message was delivered did the three-day limit on spiritual attachment start its count down. While I was apprehensive about my father's reaction, I was even more concerned about my spiritual well being.

I sat across the now cleared dinner table from him. We were the only two sitting. My wife stood behind me and my sister and her husband, John stood off to the left.

"I have something to tell you," I said cautiously. He looked at me without any facial expression.

"I have a message for you," I continued. "I have a message for you from Grandma." There was still no change in his expression. If you knew my father, this stoic reaction would seem in character. At least he was calmly listening.

"I got a message from Grandma yesterday and she asked me to give it to you," I continued. She said, "Tell Nathan, my son, that I loved him, but that I couldn't show it because his two brothers took everything I had." The room was dead quiet. I don't think anyone breathed for several seconds, which seemed like minutes. My father sat back in his chair and characteristically changed the subject. "You know when I heard you wanted to tell me something, I thought you were going to tell me you had cancer, or something."

At this point everybody was starting to relax into normality. The conversation dallied on a few mundane subjects, then abruptly my father leaned across the table to me and tapped his middle finger on the table repeatedly. A gesture he often used when he was ready to make a point. "I know what you said is true. I've always known what you said was true, but I never told anyone. So I know it came from Mama."

Later, in the driveway, my father and I shared a rare embrace. I had delivered a psychologically healing message to a 75-year-old man who had never heard his mother tell him she loved him. It was to be the first of many similar experiences of mercy that God would use me to deliver.

The next couple of days are a blur in my memory. I was still obsessed with trying to come to grips with what had happened to me. I was so engrossed and fearful that time lost any meaning to me. My wife kept me grounded as I tried to deal with what was happening.

Friday morning and afternoon came and went. That evening our oldest grandson, who was then five, came to spend his usual Friday night with his Mimi and Grandpa. As bed time drew near Carroll Ann suggested that, since he was sick with a cold, I might get a better night's sleep in the guest bedroom because she would probably be up with him most of the night.

I eased into sleep that night, not thinking of anything memorable. On a couple of occasions I heard Carroll Ann pass by the door attending to our grandson. About 3 a.m. I was awake lying on my back. I remember looking at the clock. I lay there looking at the vaulted ceiling when suddenly I felt a tingling that started in the toes of both my feet and proceeded to move up through my feet, ankles, legs, thighs, hips, torso, chest, neck and then out the top of my head. This was followed by the same tingling coming in through the top of my head and making its way down the same path and out the tips of my toes. My body was alive with tingling energy from my head to my toes. I knew that I was having a direct contact with God, which made this really weird. I thought, "How could these two experiences go on simultaneously?" Some sort of spirit attachment, which I had always been taught was of Satan, and the presence of God at the same time. And so, I called on God to take this unknown spirit. The process was repeated over and over again. I was awake. I knew there was a battle for my soul going on, but I was not frightened. Jim had said that they would be taken whether they wanted to go or not. "They will be drug out if they have to be." As these energy surges went on I continued to call on God and there would be a rush of energy and a person's name would repeatedly come into my mind and then there would be another rush of energy and this went on and on, back and forth and back and forth as I lay there in a state of almost suspended animation. I made no attempt to move, only to observe the sensations I was experiencing. I wanted these spirits gone. I knew it was not my Grandma and Grandpa that were resisting. It had to be the unidentified spirit. I knew that deep within me the angels of God were doing battle with the entity for possession of my soul. Finally it seemed as if it was over. It was over.

It seemed like it went on for 10 minutes, but as I reflect on the passage of time I realize that it was probably more like two or three minutes. It was repeated enough for me to know that I was not sleeping nor was it a figment of my imagination. When it stopped I was left with an unawareness that perplexed me. I could not remember the name I had been hearing over and over again during the episode. I lay there talking to God for almost two hours, wondering, tossing and turning, mumbling and asking Him "What was this all about? Who was the entity that would not leave? Why did it come to me? Why did it not want to leave? What effect had it had on me, and now that it was gone, how would I feel?"

I got up and went downstairs for a glass of milk. I crossed paths with my wife as she was attending to our grandson. I did not mention the episode. The last time I saw on the face of the clock was just before 5 a.m. I drifted off to sleep still asking those questions.

I awoke from a prophetic dream. It was about 5:30 a.m. and I knew immediately the answers to all my questions. I immediately got up and walked softly into our bedroom. Carroll Ann had been up most of the night with our grandson and, as God would have it, her sleep went undisturbed. I went to my closet and reached down and picked up the red toolbox. I stood up with it, turned and headed down the stairs and out onto the backyard patio. It was still dark. Almost twilight. I knew what I had to do. I opened the toolbox and started the gas grill. I began ripping the pornographic books and burning them on the grill. I burned the books and I burned the films. It went on for at least two hours.

At one point, shortly after daybreak, Carroll Ann came to the back door and asked me "what are you doing?" Only to have her question answered by seeing the open familiar toolbox and the burning flames.

It was over, and as Jim had said, "you will get a clear physical sign when it is over that will leave no doubt that all of the spirits are gone."

Later that morning I made an audiotape of the dream and my awareness of what it meant. That evening my wife and I met with my sister Mary and her husband. Below is a transcript of that meeting and of the tape I made of the dream.

I began speaking to my family.

"I talked to Jim Meade about what happened last night. He said the third entity probably did leave. He said I should tell you about the dream and then we should all talk about this as a group. I gave him a summary of what happened and he is going to see me at 8:30 next Tuesday and see if, in fact, the entity has gone.

Jim said, a real possession as far as the Catholic Church is concerned would be where I had made a conscious contract with the spirit to use my body, which I did not do. So he doesn't think that this is anything more than just a "hold over" or possibly what he terms an "attachment."

NOTE; In research for this book I have found the Catholic Church, is commonly acknowledged as the most experienced in dealing with spiritual entity possessions or attachments. There are three phases that occur for the condition to be accepted as a true possession. First is association, the second is direct influence on the host and the third and final condition is when the entity takes over the host, called the crossover. Given these conditions, my spiritual experiences would be considered "attachments" by the Catholic church, however in general Protestant and Biblical terminology, the term possession would be an appropriate description.

As my meeting with my family continued I began playing the tape I had made earlier of the dream.

The Prophetic Dream

In the dream I am walking up to a house. There is someone with me but I do not see or recognize anyone. It is a feeling that someone is helping me and I am being led to this house. It is not a mansion, but rather a nice well built home of medium size. As we walk into the house I am amazed and excited about how perfect it seems to be in every detail. The walls are all freshly painted with light neutral colors and sparkling white glossy painted trim. I move around the house running my hands over the walls and trim, expressing my pleasure at how beautifully well kept the house is. The floors are immaculately clean. I find myself looking in the corners and marveling aloud at how fantastic everything is. Still I never see who is with me, but there is a presence. I begin to talk about how perfect this will be as a home for my family and me. I am walking around from room to room. At some point I open the back door to look out. In the dream I do not see what is outside, only that my reaction is just as pleasant about the backyard as the rest of the house. "This will be a perfect place to raise my family," I tell what I perceive to be my real estate agent.

At this point I am so excited that I tell the agent that I would like to go and get my wife and bring her to see this great house. As I leave I am momentarily distracted over to my left by the presence of an old helicopter that has landed in a weeded field. Standing next to the helicopter is a young man who looks like he may have come out of the movie <u>West</u> <u>Side</u> <u>Story</u>, dressed In faded blue jeans and a white tee shirt. He is just sort of looking at me. I only glance for a moment but I get an uneasy feeling about him. He exudes a sinister feeling that makes me feel squeamish. I am so excited about the house that I dismiss the scene and hurry off to find Carroll Ann.

In the next scene in the dream, Carroll Ann and I have returned to the house. Only now the house is totally different. It is full of all kinds of skuzzy people. Some are big, some small, some black and some white, but they are all skuzzy. That's the only way I can describe them. They are nasty looking. These people are walking all around us but they aren't paying any attention to us. The house is full of them but they make no attempt to bother us.

I am filled with a sense of disappointment. The beautifully kept house is now in total disarray. I make my way back around the house as I did earlier. Now the floor is littered with garbage and dirt. The linoleum flooring is turned up in the corners. The trim is dark and stained with grime. Some windowpanes are broken. My feeling is that the owner of the house had given me this house to use and somehow in my brief absence it had been nearly demolished. It comes to me that I had left the back door unlocked when I looked out at the backyard. That moment of carelessness when I did not take care, had allowed these skuzzy people and garbage to infest this once beautiful home.

At some point the dream setting changes. My wife and I are in bed and all of a sudden this attractive young man shows up in our bedroom. I can't really see him and he is not threatening. We are not having sex but we are in bed together. The young man wants me to touch him. Not on his genitals, but to just touch him. I say "this doesn't mean anything to me." He replies, "Go ahead and see. Just go ahead and touch me and see." So I touch him and I became sexually aroused and he positions himself for me to penetrate him and I started to and then I say "no this is not right. This is not right. This is not right." And immediately he is gone. He is just gone. So there is no sex in the dream. He is just suddenly gone.

The dream now returns to the house and what is going on in the house. I take my wife outside and tell her "we've got to get rid of these people. This house is being torn up. Go back and call the house and say you are the agent who is coming with the owner. Perhaps this will make these people leave." "Ok, I'll do that," she replies. So she leaves to make the call and I turn around to face the house and all of these unbelievable nasty looking people. I mean they are just nasty, God, they are nasty looking. They have no shirts and are just nasty. All of a sudden they are coming out of the doors and windows of the house and they are getting into these old dilapidated cars. I know that somebody has to pay for this damage. Somebody has got to pay for this. I've got insurance so I kind of have the feeling it isn't going to cost me anything, but somebody has got to pay for this damage.

I have to look over a hill to see if I can get a license plate number, and there are no license plates on the cars. There are no plates on these cars. Suddenly the cars just start leaving. They go into this field and suddenly vanish into thin air. They vanish into the tall weeds. And there, hovering over the field is the same old helicopter I had seen earlier in the dream. Now it is hovering over an old, empty, shanty house and the young man is hanging onto a rope ladder and just looking at me. And then he too disappears. And I lay there and say to myself "this is over, it's time to wake up, the dream is over." And I woke up.

Below is my interpretation of the dream as I continued to play the tape for my family.

I knew instantly what the dream meant and the identity of the fourth spirit. The house was my body. I knew the beautiful, new, and well kept house was my body that had been my gift from God and my parents. It was clean and spotless when I received it. The agent was my guardian angel who always had been with me. When I left the back door open, I had allowed sin to enter into my life in the form of pornography. The skuzzy people and garbage that I had allowed to infiltrate my body, mind and soul in the form of pornographic material had eaten away at the fabric of my "house." I realized that the owner of the house (God), would be terribly angry at me for allowing this house He had given me to be so abused. My wife had been there with me and she had tried to help.

The scene in the bedroom was the moment of truth when I connected the open field, the young man, the last ditch invitation to entice me into an overt homosexual act and the choice I made to reject it. When I rejected the offer the spirit lost its grasp on me and his instant disappearance in the dream symbolized that he had been taken from me as was foretold.

When I awoke I knew that the fourth entity was the young seducer who had been killed in an automobile accident when I was 25 and he was 31. It was between the births of our son and daughter. It was at that time that I began to read the pornography. I remembered using the words many times to my wife. "Reading this doesn't mean anything to me." I would say this when she would confront me with this addiction. Now the words in the dream were another piece of the puzzle coming together. His presence in my aura prevented me from ever having a close relationship with any woman, including my own daughter, after the age of 25. It was all tied together and I understood the moment I awoke from the dream.

The tape of the dream was over and our family meeting continues on page 62.

As the years have unfolded I have come to understand the feeling I had that "somebody is going to have to pay for this damage." I believe that someone was my daughter. In the world of spirituality or the pure metaphysical it could be repayment of bad karma, or it could be her soul's agreement with God, for atonement of my sins.

Biblically, David and Bathsheba's first child dies in payment for David's sin (2 Samuel 13:13-14). The disciples ask Jesus, "Lord is this man blind because of his sins or his parents?" (John 9:2).

I am a firm believer that souls and God have "missions" known only to them, and the soul agrees to undertake these missions during their earthly lifetime(s). I use the plural because personally I am not predisposed either way. I know the soul always makes its way back to God, but it is not outside my belief structure that a soul can make multiple trips to the earth and take different bodily forms. Much like Jesus did after He arose from the tomb and appeared in multiple forms to the disciples (Mark16:12). Perhaps Jesus did this to demonstrate the very point that we are spiritual beings and the bodily appearance has no real value in the overall scheme of things.

In (Matthew 17:10-13) Jesus himself talks to his disciples about the reincarnation of Elias as John the Baptist. Are we to think that only the prophets before and during Jesus' time on earth were capable of reincarnation? Hardly, if you believe in The Living God.

I continued talking to my family and below is the transcript of that conversation.

I'm going to say this, and even though is on tape I don't want it talked about, because what you are about to hear is the dark side of my life. (Sigh.) When I was a seven-year old child I was sexually seduced by a 12, or 13-year-old male, and I never felt it to be unpleasant. On the contrary I enjoyed it. It was not a forceful thing. It was just a natural thing that happened to me. It may not have gone on for a long time, but as a child of seven it seemed like it went on for an extended period. Then it abruptly ended.

My mother was aware of it and I'm sure my father was too. It always stayed with me. It affected my entire life. I never had any further physical contact with any male, and I never had any real desire to be with a male as far as a relationship, but I never got over the experience. There was an enjoyment there.

Another male introduced me to sex. That's the long and short of it. That person died when I was about 25 years old. My mother called me in Chicago one night and while we were talking she told me he had died.

That is the end of the tape.

The next few days and weeks were bitter sweet for me. I remember calling my daughter and son to our home on separate occasions and apologizing to each of them for what I had done, and for what I had failed to do as a father. I told each of them that it was their responsibility as parents to be better for their children than I was for them. It is the obligation of each succeeding generation to learn from their parents' mistakes. My father had often said, "I only knew to do what my parents had done to me." when on rare occasions, he was confronted with his parental shortcomings. I knew that answer would not be my legacy. I had made a tragic mistake. There was nothing that could change the reality of that fact. The only thing I could do was to apologize to my wife and children and encourage my children not to use my shortcoming as their excuse. At this point it was not evident to any of us the emotional damage the years of my pornographic addiction had inflicted on my daughter's life. So as the years have gone by I have come to believe the feeling in the dream that "someone will have to pay for this damage" may have fallen on my daughter. There would be many years of painful restructuring of our relationship that would begin sooner than either one of us could imagine.

CHAPTER 5
THE REALITY OF THE
SPIRITUAL WORLD

The weeks and months that followed were intertwined with periods of every emotion I could possibly imagine. At times I was at peace, and at times I literally thought I was loosing my mind. The one overriding desire was to learn the truth of what I had experienced. I knew what I had been through was real. The question was, "Is this of God or is this of Satan?" Throughout the experiences described in this chapter my only desire was to bring myself closer to experiencing the truth. There was fear in pursuing the truth and yet something inside me told me that I had to move forward. I had to pursue the truth about the spiritual world. For I knew that is where God resided, and therefore it was the better way to experience Him and to know Him.

There are some Christian religious denominations that will say without hesitation that spiritual contact must be satanic. That is simply not true. The Bible is full of passages that relate to direct experiences of humans with God, angels and dreams that were prophetic. I simply made my wishes totally clear. If it was not of God I wanted nothing to do with it. There are many books written on protecting one's self from the darkness. As I reflect on my experiences I believe God blessed and protected me and allowed me to experience the paranormal for reasons that will become clear later in this book. In other words, I believe my experiences were the Will of God for me. Not all of them involved contact with the good side. I am not recommending that anyone follow my path. We each must follow our own path. As Jesus says to Peter as to what John should do, "If I ask that he wait here for my return, what is that to thee? Follow thou me now." (John 21:22).

The first book I read on the metaphysical was entitled *The Way of the Peaceful Warrior* by Dan Millman, a former Olympic gymnast. The book is an adventure story about a young college student who is mentored by a supposed elderly service station attendant, only to learn he is much more than that. He teaches Dan to embrace the mysteries of life and, more importantly, the mysteries of the spiritual world. In the metaphysical he might be considered the physical manifestation of a spiritual guide, in Christianity, an angel of God.

The second book was the sequel entitled *No Ordinary Moments*. These two books were simple and easy to read about how the conscious and subconscious minds work together and the basic significance of accessing the spiritual world.

By the end of the second book I was fascinated. For some 12 to 15 years I had been developing my own theology of who God was, and where He resided. I truly felt my theology was unique. Now I found that I was not unique, but there were a host of people in the world who thought much like I did and wrote about it. I devoured approximately 36 books on the metaphysical and paranormal in the subsequent 15 months. I could almost speed read these books and absorb everything I read, much like an electronic scanner. It was a steady parade of "yeah, yeah, and umhums" as I knowingly absorbed the written information.

The one prevalent aspect of the metaphysical I did not embrace was "channeling." I define this as the process of consciously making contact with a spirit and allowing that spirit to enter your being for the purpose of using your physical facilities to transmit information to yourself, and or others. I am not totally sure why I was so leery of this at the time, but I believe that it was because I had been conversing with God for the previous dozen years, so the thought of now embracing Moses, Isaiah, Abraham, or some unknown spirit for information seemed rather absurd. Later I would come to be thankful that I had not embraced and allowed this invasion, though the struggle for my mind would still occur.

The purpose of this book is not to preach, nor to judge. However I would be remiss if I did not, on occasions, point out signposts that can be potential hazardous to your mental and spiritual health. I know several people who channel spirits. They would have a totally different viewpoint than me. My only warning to a novice is that it is not difficult to access the spiritual world. It is done everyday by both good and evil humans. To my knowledge, there is no way for a human to discern the good from the evil spirits until after the fact.

In one way the spiritual world is no different than our physical world. There are good people, not so good people and down right evil persons. One runs the same risk in the spiritual world. The problem is that humans cannot discern the good or evil of a spirit except by the results they produce. Much like the insidious pornography that I thought was not bothering me, or meant anything to me, a lesser spirit can very slowly infect the mental and discernment processes. Fore warned is fore armed. Beware and proceed with caution. As I point out later in this book, accessing the spiritual world brought me closer to God. God does not expect to come to us and then have us sit in a corner. In the Gospels Jesus asks us to "come follow Me." As God incarnate as a man, Jesus sought after the Will of His Father. In the study of the Gospels we see Jesus grow in the knowledge of the Father's Will for Him. The most commonly known event is His 40 days in the desert fasting and seeking the Will of the Father, and his subsequent encounter with Satan. Following these temptations He begins His public ministry.

The two weeks following the exorcism of my four spirits were full of more spiritual experiences. My daughter and sister saw Jim several times. I only witnessed one of my daughter's sessions, and though I was a novice, God allowed me to see that she too was under the control of a negative spirit. I knew that my daughter harbored a spirit, or spirits, that did not have her best interests at heart. For reasons that will become known to the reader later, Jim did not detect the significance of their presence.

It was one evening after witnessing the session with my daughter that my wife and I were sitting in our den. She was reading and I was contemplating my daughter's session with Jim. The more I thought about what I had seen the more distraught I became. I had only recently been lifted out of the mire of my own attachments, and here I was faced with the reality of my daughter's problem. In her session she had said that she had a friend with her who was there to help her. My intuition told me that I should be concerned. Why had Jim not perceived the negative presence? Was this "friend" the negative presence I sensed? I began praying and asking God to tell me what this was all about. I was getting no answer. Finally I lost my composure. I spoke to God forcefully. "I want a sign from You, tell me if this entity is of good or evil, and I want it now!!!!"

I held a small yellow pad in my lap and a pen in my right hand. Suddenly my right hand began to move. Something was happening. I knew my hand was moving without my consciously moving it. I had been looking up as I spoke to God in the strongest emotion

I could muster. When the drawing started I slowly allowed my head to lower and my eyes to fall on the yellow pad. What I saw was a continuous, jagged, sawtooth line that my hand was drawing on the pad. I was immediately aware that I was not doing this, and further I had no idea what was being drawn. To me it resembled a jagged sine wave (see Figure 1). Being technically inclined, I thought it might be some scientific message. I simply let it continue. It went on for several minutes. When it was over I looked at it from every angle. I saw nothing that I could identify. I slowly got up, still trying to make something of the weird drawing, and took it across the room to my wife. Without any indication as to how I drew the picture, asked her if she knew what the picture was. Without hesitation she said "It's a wolf." Terror struck my heart. To me a wolf was something to fear - a predator. I quickly related to my wife how I had come about the drawing. As was the case throughout my many months of upheaval, my wife remained calm for both of us.

Figure 1

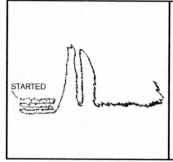

	This was the position of the pad of paper when I started the automatic drawing. See the upper left-hand corner "started".
STARTED	Turn the page 1/4 turn clock wise. That is how everyone saw the "wolf."

I called my sister and asked if we could come over to their home. She said yes. I walked in the door and placed the drawing in front of both of them. Each said without hesitation, "a wolf." I reached my daughter by phone and asked her what a wolf meant to her. She said in American Indian folklore the wolf was a sign of protection. She, in fact, had acquired a German Shepard for that very reason. I asked her and her husband to come to her aunt's home and see the drawing. She did, and she and her husband both indicated the drawing looked like a wolf. She felt the message was positive, and to her it would have been, but I was the one who asked for the sign and the drawing was sent to me. I said nothing more about the drawing to her. She was leaving within a few days to start graduate school in Colorado. It was now the middle of June 1993.

It was only two or three weeks later that I was still struggling with the reality of my experiences. I routinely walked our neighborhood for exercise. Now as I walked, I pondered my experiences, and talked with God. One afternoon I had been particularly persistent with my talking to God. "Please send me a sign that confirms to me these experiences are of You." I prayed the entire hour I walked. When I returned to our home I promptly set down in one of the front porch chairs and leaned back and closed my eyes in relaxation. There in my closed eye vision was a picture like none I had ever seen, or have seen since. This was not a fuzzy image. This was as clear as any color TV picture you can imagine.

71

There was a perfectly round ball that was as black as black can be: as black as pitch. Around the perimeter and behind the black ball was the slightest hint of a golden hue. (See figure 2A.) Later I saw a still picture of an eclipse of the sun. It was the closest thing to the vision that I have ever seen. From the center of the circle curving over to 2 o'clock was a thin golden string. As I continued to watch the vision, the string began to move in a clockwise motion (See Figure 2B.) As it did the black was slowly uncovered and replaced by the golden antique color that was hidden under the black circle. The clockwise uncovering continued until all that remained was a perfectly round and magnificent golden ball. (See figure 2C.)

I continued to examine the picture in detail. I noticed that the center of the ball was comprised of a small jagged opening that was a vivid purple in color. I focused on the center and realized it was pulsing. Very slowly it would slightly open and then contract. This procedure continued to repeat itself. I thought the purple center would open like a flower to reveal even more of itself, but it simply continued to open and close in a pulsing manner. I continued for several minutes to take in the beauty of the golden ball that had an antique-like surface texture. After several minutes the vision disappeared.

Sliver of Gold

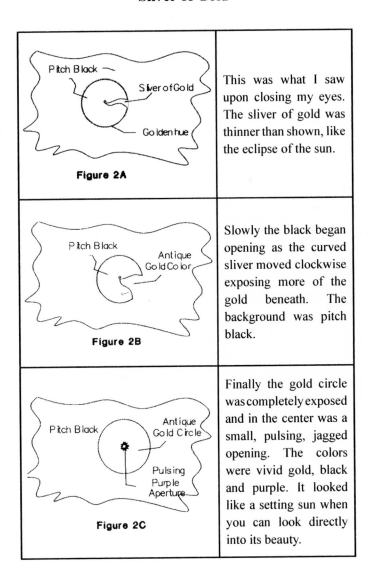

This was what I saw upon closing my eyes. The sliver of gold was thinner than shown, like the eclipse of the sun.

Figure 2A

Slowly the black began opening as the curved sliver moved clockwise exposing more of the gold beneath. The background was pitch black.

Figure 2B

Finally the gold circle was completely exposed and in the center was a small, pulsing, jagged opening. The colors were vivid gold, black and purple. It looked like a setting sun when you can look directly into its beauty.

Figure 2C

I was now even further perplexed. What did this vision mean and where did it come from? The only conclusive thing I could say about the vision was that it was the most beautiful picture I had ever seen. I remember cautiously revealing the vision to a few persons with their only reaction being strange looks. Finally one young man said, "I only know that Satan is the liar of all liars, and that this surely came from him." I immediately shut down any contact with the spiritual world. Each time I would have one of these experiences I would pursue outside counsel and as soon as I heard something negative I would immediately withdraw. I am not saying that was wrong. As time progressed I would take two steps forward, then one large step backwards. It is difficult to explain the feeling that one has after one has experienced the reality of the spiritual world. It is one thing to intellectually know it, it is totally something else to live it. This battle is described further below. As I look back I could see there was yet another spiritual battle for my mind to endure.

One thing I was sure of was the conspicuous absence of any desire on my part to read pornography. When I had revealed my dark side to my 30-year-old son, his singular most significant advice to me was "replace the void you have created with something good, lest the evil return to fill that space again." That advice stayed with me although it was much later that I became aware of the biblical significance (Matthew 12:43-45).

As the summer of 1993 unfolded, I was still experiencing significant physical pain as well as this emotional trauma. As I pursued my spirituality I was still enduring a distinct lack of full energy. I was now perhaps up to 75 percent of my former self. My wheat intolerance was growing worse by the week. Any intake of wheat products gave me a tremendous onset of gastritis that would persist for days. I was on Zantac, and an anti-acid reflux medication, neither of which was very effective. The only good thing about not eating wheat was the fact that I had no trouble staying at 170 pounds. At six feet tall, and with my build, I was always greeted with the question "have you been sick, Nathan?" When one eliminates wheat from the diet, that will include bread, pasta, cookies, cakes and pies. I could drink no alcohol, even wine irritated my stomach and esophagus. It is rather amazing how many products we consume that are wheat or grain based, or contain some amounts of wheat. In my mind I felt that if I did not overcome this stomach irritation I would surely end up with stomach cancer as had my mother before me.

During the summer and early fall of 1993 I was devouring books on the metaphysical. The summer turned into fall and Jim Meade came to Memphis again in October. I saw him a couple of times, still trying to find the cause of my stomach problem, but to no avail. There were no further spiritual entity possession problems. We had become friends and he taught me much about the metaphysical. At one point he mentioned he would see me when he returned to Memphis in January of '94. I told him that since 1991 my wife and I had spent Januarys in the Sarasota area. We always stayed on Long Boat Key at an older, but well kept resort. He related that he had a good friend, Dr. Richard Schulman, who was one of his protégés, who lived in Sarasota. Richard was a clinical psychologist who had taken up the use of hypnosis as part of his practice. He also told me about Mary Park, a mystic who lived in a small town near Sarasota. He suggested that I look them up when I was down there. I agreed, not really knowing if I would, or how much each would play in the unraveling of my spirituality.

The last two months of 1993 were relatively quiet. I continued to uneventfully read and study the metaphysical and looked forward to our five-week Florida vacation beginning in late December and continuing into early February of 1994. As October gave way to November I began to experience a strange and unwanted occurrence. As my days unfolded I would become aware of a name coming into my mind with no predictable frequency. The name I began to hear in my mind was Jesus Christ.

It is important for the reader to realize that at this time I was not receptive to a change in my manner of communication with God. Since 1983 I had been contemplating and talking with God on a regular basis. I would ask Him about everything, ranging from His identity to helping me make business decisions. It was in 1983 that my life took its first conscious step towards a meaningful union with God.

I had started my environmental consulting and testing business in the summer of 1972. As the years went by and our clientele base expanded, I often found myself driving up to a hundred miles one way to visit a client and then returning to Memphis. The 200-mile round trip would easily require four to five hours of driving, depending on the road conditions. During many of these trips when the current client business thinking was completed, I would often sort out long-range business decisions, or contemplate God. Those lengthy car conversations were my first real attempt in learning who He was, and where He resided.

By 1982 we had been in business for 10 years and had been reasonably successful. I began to have a strange feeling that I was supposed to do something, but I could not put my finger on what it was. As the months slipped by I found that this urge had something to do with "giving back" in gratitude for my financial success. In the fall of 1983 at Sunday mass the priest gave a homily and said, "We are all called to feed the hungry and clothe the naked." Those words were like a light going on inside me. I knew in that moment I was being called to help feed the hungry. I was so excited that I could hardly contain myself. The next day I called the rectory at 8:01 a.m. and the priest who had given the homily just happened to answer the telephone. I told him how moved I had been by his words and that

I knew God was talking to me about feeding the poor. I asked him "how can I get started?" From the other end of the phone came a very detached response "We don't have any poor people in our parish." I was stunned, but something told me to let it go. I politely ended the conversation and hung up the phone. Moments later I was irritated. I knew that this is what God wanted me to do. How could he have talked about helping the poor on Sunday, and be so detached the next morning? I looked up three other Catholic churches in the telephone book and called them. To my utter amazement each priest gave me the same response in the exact same words: "We don't have any poor people in our parish." At the end of the fourth call I was totally perplexed. I couldn't understand what was going on. Later I related the incident to a long time friend of mine who told me I should call a local monsignor, which I did. He was most receptive to my wanting to help the poor and thus began a long-term relationship and the beginning of my bartering with God. My relationship with Monsignor Paul Clunan continued until he retired and finally passed away.

During this period I began to send small amounts of money to the monsignor for use in helping the poor. I had always envisioned helping the "newly poor," people who had worked most of their lives and then unexpectedly through no fault of their own, had suddenly become unemployed and needed help. The good monsignor had something else in mind. He was sending my contributions into the inner city poor. I started to question him about his use of our money, but God put into my mind that my call was to furnish the money to the priest. It was clear that I was being told to let him use the money the way he felt was best. It was the beginning of my learning to "let go and let God." I did not know it at the time but this was my first experience with being "part of the Body of Christ."

Like St. Thomas in the Bible, I still had my doubts this was what God was calling me to do. So as time went on I would increase the amount of money I sent for the poor. I would always accompany that increase with the prayer to God, "if this is what I am supposed to do, you will have to provide the means for me to continue at this new level." I can tell you that God responded just as He promises He will. We had reached a point we were sending Msgr. Clunan a significant amount of money. I would write all the checks for the month including this rather large one for the poor. Then I would balance the checkbook. In a stretch of 18 months, on at least a dozen occasions I would find a non-recorded deposit, or an addition mistake that was almost identical to the amount of the check I had written to Monsignor Clunan. Effectively, when I had finished writing all of the checks, the amount sent to the poor had not changed the amount of money left in our account. It was God's way of providing for us and letting me know I was on the right track.

I often bartered with Him. We once were bidding on a large government contract. When the bids were opened we were the 24th highest bidder, not likely to be in contention for the award. I told God that if we got that contract I would give the poor 25 percent of our profits. As the government evaluation continued there was a government request for a price extension faxed to all of the bidders over a long holiday weekend. Twelve of the bidders in front of us failed to acknowledge the faxed request and were disqualified. Now we were 12th on the list. As several months went by, bidders were eliminated for lack of technical qualifications. At the end of 18 months of evaluations, the 11 in front of us were technically eliminated. Our company was awarded the largest five-year contract in our history.

I knew that God was listening to me and responding to my bartering. It was years later that I realized there was Biblical precedence. God enjoys a good bartering and conversation as we journey through this life headed back to him. Genesis 18 relates how Abraham bartered with God in trying to save Sodom. Thus began a 10-year relationship with God that involved my talking to Him, asking for His help, insisting on His help, if He wanted me to carry out His Will because I knew I didn't have the resources to do it alone.

Now unexpectedly, 10 years later in the fall of 1993, I began getting the name Jesus Christ into my mind. The thought was that I should be praying and talking to Jesus too. This perplexed me because at this point I did not consciously perceive God as a Trinity, although my Catholic education certainly had taught me about the Father, Son and Holy Ghost. I was thinking God the Father and Creator, who was my main man, the One I turned to when I needed help and comfort and support. I was concerned that God would be ticked off if I suddenly introduced this Jesus Christ into the picture. I really didn't know how he would fit into the conversation pattern. It sort of reminded me of working directly for the president of a company and then being informed that from now on I needed to come through the VP. It led me to feel anxious about my relationship with God. I realize that now, from a Christian viewpoint, that logic sounds hilarious, but that was just another leg in the weird journey God had orchestrated for me.

This lack of knowledge about Jesus has been a source of bewilderment. My wife and I were born and raised Catholics, which of course included 12 years of parochial education that was saturated with Catechism classes. Yet the neither one of us realized the significance of who Jesus Christ was. This was strange because six years later I have become aware of my religion and I see Jesus as the focus of the mass and all of the sacraments. Perhaps it was just a veil over my consciousness that forced me down a road that God knew I needed to take.

The gift of giving was born in me. I am still driven by the phrase "An empty stomach can hear nothing good, much less the Word of God."

Specifically to those Christians who have read this far, I commend you as Truth Seekers. I would summarize for you two things that have happened to this point and should encourage your persistence to continue reading. When Jesus is accused of exorcising demons in the name of Satan, He refutes that notion with the insight that, if that were true, Satan would be destroying himself, since "a house divided cannot stand" (Matthew 12:26). Eight years since the expulsion of the negative spirit, I have had no reoccurrence of desire to read, or in any fashion, entertain, pornography.

Secondly, how would the onset of the name Jesus Christ unexplainably entering my thoughts benefit Satan's cause? It was not obvious to me at the time, but as the next few months unfolded I became aware that someone other than Satan was residing within me. In the following chapters I will explain how I found out who that someone is.

CHAPTER 6
PAST LIVES

The day after Christmas 1993, Carroll Ann and I put our Lincoln Towncar on the road and headed to Florida for our annual five week winter hiatus. I could put it on autopilot and it sort of drove itself. We would stop overnight in Tallahassee at the Days Inn. It was easy for us to fall into a routine when we traveled to the same place over and over again. We stopped here for gas and there for a Dairy Queen, and so on. Man is a creature of habit, and after a while, it would take 25 percent longer to reach our ultimate destination.

We stayed in a Gulf-side condo for a week with our longtime Canadian friends, Jim and Jill. They departed for home a week later and we had the place to our selves. The relaxing days turned into weeks. I have categorized one week of vacation as time off, two weeks as a vacation, and three weeks or more as a change in life style. I once asked my brother-in-law, who had been out of work for six months, if he ever got bored. He replied "No, the concept that people have to work to be happy is a myth perpetrated by business owners."

While window shopping in Sarasota near the end of January, my wife spotted a flyer in a book store window advertising an evening seminar on hypnotism. She suggested we attend and see what it was about. I scanned down the flyer and not surprisingly, found the name Dr. Richard Schulman, the man my friend Jim Meade had recommended I visit while we were on vacation. I said nothing to Carroll Ann about this and later that evening we went to the seminar. It was fun and educational. There was a good-sized crowd of about 50 persons of all ages and cultures. We settled in as Richard sat on a stool in the middle of the group and began talking about practicing clinical psychology for over 10 years in the conventional manner, and how frustrating it had been for him. Often he had seen clients for years with no definitive improvement. Now that he had learned this new technique he had cured many people. Some patients reported significant improvement or cures after only one or two visits.

He told the story of how one rainy night he found himself driving from California to Arizona, and ending up at Jim Meade's door at 2:00 a.m. He talked about how Jim had taught him the art of hypnosis and it had changed his professional, and eventually his personal, life.

The seminar continued with Richard leading us through a relaxation meditation. Later he asked for volunteers in the audience to participate in a hypnotic past life regression. A past life regression is the belief structure that follows reincarnation. Those who embrace reincarnation believe that if your soul has been to earth on previous occasions you obviously would have what are called "past lives." There can be bad karma (negative energy) between two persons who have traveled through past lives together, often referred to as "soul mates." There can be residual negative energy from traumatic incidents in past lives that souls have not fully released, and those incidents cause physical and psychological problems in one's current life by affecting the subconscious.

Two young ladies volunteered for the hypnotic demonstration. I cannot relate to you the specifics, but I remember they were very satisfied with their brief but effective sessions. Observing his work that evening, I intuitively knew that he could help me with my stomach problem. Where Jim Meade was a hypnotist and intuitive without peer, his specialty was spiritual possessions or attachments. Richard had the combination of 10 years clinical psychology experience, intuition, and mastery of hypnosis. The combination was powerful. That evening I made an appointment with him for early the next week. It was now late in January.

Having been previously hypnotized, I had little trouble settling into the session with Richard. We talked briefly about why I was there and the problems I was dealing with physically and emotionally. Twenty minutes after

I arrived he began, and below is a transcript of that session on January 24, 1994.

Richard's office is quiet and filled with pleasant background music and ocean surf sounds. I sat in a recliner with my shoes and glasses removed. My head and arms rested comfortably on the upholstered chair. He has a pleasant melodic and soothing voice.

(Richard begins.) *"A teacher of mine says that the shortest distance between two points is an intention. Nathan, I want you to begin our work together by silently, to yourself, stating your intention for this work."* (There is a pause and as always I state my intention that I want to be protected by God and that He will bless this work. If it is His Will I will be relieved of my chronic gastritis.)

"And once you have done that I want you to acknowledge and honor a part of yourself very deep and very wise, that part of you that loves and guides you. Some people call this part the Inner Healer, some call it the Subconscious Mind, or the Inner Physician. From my prospective it doesn't matter what you call it, what matters is that you acknowledge and honor that part of yourself that is very deep and very wise, that part that loves, protects, and guides you." (Pause. I believe that the Spirit of God resides within me. The God within me, and I ask that He guide us in this session.)

"And now that you have done that, I want you to look at a few ideas. Ordinarily the breath is automatic, involuntary. This is good. Imagine for a moment that each and every breath that you take had to be voluntary and controlled by your conscious awareness. This wouldn't leave very much time for anything else. Still, it leaves us with a question. How do we survive? How do we live? How do we breath? I think we are able to do this because of that deeper part of us, that part very deep and very wise part that loves, protects and guides us. The Subconscious Mind, or The Inner Healer. I want you to start to connect with that deeper part. It is fortunate that the breath is probably the easiest physiological process that can be placed under voluntary control. I want you to begin by just observing your breath, tracking your breath, the tension of the inhale, the relaxation of the exhale. Tension, followed by relaxation. Tension, followed by relaxation. You can't be tense if you are relaxed. The two responses are incompatible. They cannot exist together at the same time. In a moment I am going to ask you to take some voluntary breaths. With each and every breath you take, I want you to take yourself inside of yourself. Not giving up control, but turning the control inside. You can use any pattern of breath that you wish."

(Richard continues in a slow and melodic voice. This is the process of bringing me into an altered state, much like one would feel in meditation.)

"Begin now and take six voluntary breaths and with each and every breath that you take sink more and more deeply into the chair. Deeper, ...deeper . . and . . deeper and deeper. Relaxing and letting go. Relaxing and letting go. Deeper and deeper. Deeper and deeper still." (Pause.)

"At the end of the sixth breath cycle just rest and breath normally." (Long pause as the process unfoldes. Soft music and ocean sounds in the background.)

"Take yourself inside of yourself. As long as people have been searching for inner healing, for inner truth, people have known about the healing properties of breath. Take yourself inside now. Going deeper and deeper. Deeper and still deeper. As you relax and let go. Deeper and now deeper. Experiencing your inner self. Sinking into the chair. The chair is supporting every cell of the body as you relax and let go. Relax and you are letting go. Experiencing yourself going deeper and deeper. Deeper and deeper."

(There is a long pause and continued background music.)

"Rest normally at the end of the breathing cycle."

"I want you to now use your imagination. I want you to imagine that you are moving down a very large escalator and as you move down the escalator.

Moving down,. . down,. . down. Continuing down the escalator. Till you get to the bottom of the escalator. Going deeper and deeper as you move down. And your imagination can be a picture in your mind's eye, a sound in your mind's ear, or a feeling in your mind's heart. Use all of your inner senses if you wish. At the bottom of the escalator I want you to imagine an energy source at the top of your head. It could be in the form of a white light, or a vibration, or a tone of music. Whatever form you would like will be fine. I want you to bring this energy down through the central column of your body. Begin now. Bring it down through the head and the face, the jaw. Feel the head beginning to sink into the chair. The light continues to come down. Down through the head and face and the jaw. Down through the neck and the throat. Feel the throat gently opening as the energy moves down. Down through the heart region. Continuing down to the stomach, down through the reproductive organs and down to the base of that central column. To what some people call the root chakra."

(In the metaphysical and traditional eastern religions there are seven chakras or energy centers. The top of the head, the middle of the forehead, the throat, the heart, the solar plexus, the stomach and the base of the tail bone. The one at the base of the tailbone is called the root chakra.)

"Allow this energy to move through the central column like a river. For this energy, this universal energy exists

everywhere. It flows through everyone and everything, and does in fact, flow through every human being like a river."

(Pause and then he continues.)

"When that central column is filled with energy and is glowing and warm from your heart, begin visualizing the pumping of this energy throughout the remainder of the body. Touching every muscle every nerve, every fiber, every bone, every organ. Pumping energy through the shoulders, the upper arms and elbows, the forearms and wrists, and finally the hands and fingers too. Pumping energy throughout the remainder of the back, and the spine. Feel the back and the spine sinking gently into the chair. Pump it throughout the remainder of the chest and the abdomen. Then moving down through the buttocks and pelvic region. Continuing down through the upper legs and thighs, then down through the knees, calves and shins and ankles, feet and toes. Pump the energy until the entire body is filled with this energy from head to toe, toe to head, left to right, and right to left, front to back and back to front. Touching every muscle, every nerve, every fiber, every bone, and organ. Touching every cell."

(Pause. The visualization, or intention of energy movement, is core to the healing process. It is widely held at all levels of medicine that visualization of healing energy moving through a body can, at a minimum, have a placebo effect on that body. For me the energy movement is real and I experience a healing effect when the energy moves. I have written extensively about this theory in *Contemplation and the Presence of God.)*

"And when the body is filled with energy bring the energy out around the body like a halo. Know that only goodness can come through this energy and that you are perfectly safe and protected in it. Ask that God bless the work we are doing together and that God sends a cone of white light with pure sound bringing us protection, guidance, peace, love and healing. In the name of the light I command that anyone or anything that does not have Nathan's highest good in mind to leave now and to not return."

(Here we are stating our intention together that any energy imparted into my heart, mind, body and soul is energy only from God.)

"In a moment I am going to be counting backwards from ten to one. With each number that I count I want you to give yourself permission to go deeper and deeper. At the end of the count I am going to say the words "relax now" and snap my fingers and you will be in a very deep and peaceful state of hypnosis. Ten. Going deeper. Nine deeper and deeper still. Eight. Relax and let go. Seven. Experience yourself relaxing and sinking deeply into the chair. Six. The chair supports every cell of the body. Five. Relax deeply and completely. Four. Relax every muscle, every nerve,

every fiber, every bone, and every organ. Three. Relax every cell. For in each and every cell there is a little bit of your consciousness in the DNA. Two. Profound and deep relaxation, and One, relax now."

(Accompanied by the snapping of his fingers. The use of this technique allows Richard to bring me up to conscious awareness if need be and the hypnotic suggestion of responding to his finger snapping would allow me to return immediately to the altered state.)

"Each and every time you hear me say the words "relax now" and snap my fingers you will take yourself to a very deep and relaxed state of hypnosis. You will do this only in the context of our sessions, or when you are practicing the tape. Only when you hear my voice say 'relax now' and snap my fingers."

(At this point I am completely relaxed, and in a peaceful state of hypnosis or deep meditation.)

"I want you to allow the conscious mind to step aside now. Neither encourage, or discourage what will unfold. I wish to speak directly to the subconscious mind.

Subconscious mind in a moment I am going to cause you to make one of his fingers rise. Rise in the joy, peace and happiness associated with the word yes. Fill the finger with energy as if a string is pulling on it allowing it to rise and float. Subconscious mind I want you to cause a finger to rise in the joy, peace and happiness associated with the word yes, and do that now."

(Initially there is no response.)

"Finger, filling with energy is beginning to rise and float. Rise and float, rise and float... . . . yes subconscious, I understand. Okay. Very good."

(Richard continues after getting the index finger response.)

"Subconscious mind I am going to ask you now to cause a different finger to raise. A different finger. This finger to rise with the strength, power and assertiveness associated with the word no, and do that now. Yes, I understand subconscious, you may relax that finger. Subconscious what I see is the right index is for yes and right pinky is for no. If this is accurate signal me with the yes finger. Yes, I understand. Okay."

"Subconscious mind he has come to me with essentially what I see as two problems. I am not sure if they are connected. One is the chronic gastritis and one is the food allergy. Are these two problems connected?"

(Pause for a finger response.) Note: In the following transcription when a question is asked and answered "yes" or "no," the response was a finger response. When I verbally respond it is so indicated.

"Yes, okay. Subconscious, he suspected the chronic gastritis was connected to the relationship with his father. From your prospective is this accurate?" (Pause.) *"No, okay."*

"Subconscious mind I am looking for the best plan with how to deal with these allergies and gastritis and I would like to speak with his Inner Physician. Will his Inner Physician communicate with me on this topic?" (Pause.) *"Yes, okay."*

"Physician, is it preferable to address the gastritis and food allergies one at a time? Yes, okay."

"Is the top priority issue the gastritis? No."

"Is the food allergy the top priority issue? Yes, okay."

"The food allergy. Does it have its origin physiological? No, okay."

"I would like to look at the origin of the food allergy. Is the origin of the food allergy in his present lifetime? No, okay."

"Is the origin of the food allergy in a past lifetime? Yes."

"Is there more than one past lifetime that impacts the food allergies? Yes, okay."

"Are there any future lifetimes that impact the food allergies? No, okay."

"Inner Physician what I am hearing is there is more than one lifetime in the past that influences the food allergy. Nothing in the present lifetime, or any future lifetimes. From your perspective Inner Physician is this accurate? Yes, okay."

"The first past lifetime that influences the food allergies. Does it take place before the year 1500? No."

"Does it take place before the year 1800? No."

"Does it take place before the year 1850? No."

"Does it take place before the year 1875? No."

"Does it take place before the year 1900? No."

"Does it take place before the year 1925? (Pause.) Yes."

"Does it take place before the year 1910? Yes."

"Does it take place before the year 1905? Yes."

"Does it take place in 1904? Yes."

"Does it take place in Europe? Yes."

"Does it take place in England? Yes."

"Does it take place in other countries as well? Yes."

"Is the primary country it takes place in England? Yes. Okay you can relax now."

"In that past lifetime was he male? Yes."

"In that lifetime was he married? Yes."

"In order to understand the food allergy do we have to look at his occupation during that lifetime? Yes, okay."

(Short pause while Richard gathers his thoughts. Richard is intuitive and his questions are moved by that gift.)

"In order to understand this food allergy do we have to look at his death in that lifetime? Yes."

"Besides occupation and death do we have to look at any significant relationships during that lifetime? No, okay."

"Besides occupation and death are there any other significant issues we need to look at in that lifetime. No, okay."

"Let's start with occupation. Does his occupation have something to do with food? Yes, okay."

"Was he a chef? Yes, okay."

"Does this go beyond being a chef? Was he a chef for someone famous? No."

"Something happened when he was a chef that caused a very negative outcome. Yes."

"Did it cause the death of other people? Yes."

"Did it cause his own death as well? Yes, okay."

"Did something he do poison a significant number of people? Yes."

"And was he one of those people? Yes. Is this the origin of the food allergy and does it have something specifically to do with wheat? Yes. And alcohol? Yes."

"Does it have something to do with fermentation? Yes."

"Was he trying to make his own alcohol? Yes. And did something go wrong with the process and it poisoned people? Yes, okay."

"Subconscious mind I want you to block any of my expectation, thoughts or feelings. Do that now."

(Richard continues to probe.)

"What I am hearing is that his attempt to make alcohol went bad and killed himself and others. Is that accurate? Yes."

"And this is the basis for the food allergy. Is that accurate? Yes, good."

"Is he ready to let go of this? Yes, okay. Would he prefer to transform it rather than let go of it? Yes, okay."

"I want him to pick a picture, an image a word or a phrase of music. Something very beautiful to him that he would like to transfer this negative energy into, this food allergy."

(Richard pauses while I begin to envision a peaceful and secluded beach.)

"When he has made his selection please signal yes. It can be anything as long as it is beautiful to him."

"Okay just relax Nathan."

"Is the energy causing the food allergy diffused throughout his body? Yes, okay."

"I would like to transform all that energy to a word, thought or a phrase or music or sound and I want him to bring that symbol to every muscle, every fiber, nerve, every bone and every organ. Is that a little clearer? Yes."

"Is he ready to do that? Yes, okay."

"Now I want him to do this in an interesting way. I want him imagine his DNA. The spirals of the DNA and I want him to start moving down the DNA and wherever there is fear replace it with that image or symbol of love. Then send that image to every muscle, every nerve, every fiber, every bone, every organ, every liquid and every cell of the body from head to toe, toe to head, left to right, right to left, back to front, front to back. Until the entire body energy has been transformed. Like a computer that is copying a program it moves throughout the entire body. When you have completed that process signal yes." (Pause.)

"Be sure to include the non physical bodies as well. Subconscious Mind will know exactly how to do this. Working with Inner Physician will cause this to occur and make it so. Yes, I understand."

"Okay subconscious. Is there anything else we need to do in that lifetime in England in 1904? No, okay."

"Is there a lifetime, perhaps a secondary lifetime that impacts the food allergies? Yes, okay."

"Do I have permission to investigate this lifetime as well? Yes, okay."

"Did this lifetime occur before the year 1500? Yes."

"Did it occur before the year 1000? Yes."

"Did it occur before the time of Christ? Yes."

"Did it occur before 5,000 B.C? Yes."

"Did it occur before 10,000 B.C.? Yes."

"Did it occur before 25,000 B.C.? No."

"Did it occur before 15,000 B.C? Yes."

"Did it occur before 20,000 B.C.? Yes."

"What I'm hearing is that it occurred between the years 20,000 and 25,000 B.C. Yes."

"Is it important that we be more specific about this date? No."

"In that lifetime was he male? Yes."

"In that lifetime was he married? Yes."

"Is it important that we understand his occupation in that lifetime? Yes."

"Is it important that we look at his death in that lifetime? No."

"Are there any other important things to look at from that lifetime in order to completely settle the issue of the food allergies? No."

"Does his occupation in that lifetime have something to do with food? Yes, okay."

"Was he a farmer? Yes, okay."

"Did he use some pretty amazing technologies to help him in his farming? Yes."

"Are these the energy sources he has been obsessing about? Yes. "

(Richard is referring to the past 25 years of my continuous obsession on the conversion of static magnetic energy to kinetic energy.)

"Now from my perspective I don't care if he remembers the energy sources or not, but I want him to feel better. That is the only thing that matters. That he feels better. Okay. If he gets information about the energy sources okay, but the most important thing is that he feels better. "

"Did something happen with those technologies to cause a lot of food to go bad? Yes. And did it happen out of greed? Yes, okay. "

"And does he carry a lot of guilt about what happened? Yes, okay. "

"And is this connected to what he feels? "

(I start to sob audibly. In this session this is the first emotion I have shown.)

"Let it go Nathan. " (Richard interjects.)

"Is this the source of why his stomach burns when he writes the checks? Yes. "

"Let it all go Nathan. Let it all go. Let it all go for now and for all times. Let it all go. Don't block any of it. Doesn't do you any good inside. Let it all go for now and for all time. Let it all go."

(I am now sobbing uncontrollably as I feel the emotions release.)

"Yes, Let it all go. Let all of it go out of every muscle, every nerve, every fiber, every bone, and every organ, out of every cell, out of every liquid in the physical and non-physical bodies. I want you to move it all out. You are not responsible anymore. Now the issue is learning."

"Let it all go. Let it all go for now and all times."

(I begin to sob more forcefully as the pent up energy is moving.)

"Let it all go, you can do it. Don't block any of it. Okay. You've got it. Okay. I'm going to put a microphone on you now."

"Subconscious mind. Any thoughts that come up that he needs to speak to directly? Yes."

(My first response is a sigh.)

(Richard asks.) *"What are you experiencing now?"*

(I speak hesitantly.) *"I understand . . . . . why I want to help people. . . I understand why I want to give the power source to mankind."* (Still sobbing.)

"What happened?" Richard asks. *"I don't think you need to know exactly what happened. You just need to know the feeling."*

(I reply.) *"I want to give money. For some reason it is important that I give money to people. Not time, but money."*

Richard speaks to my Subconscious Mind.

"The lesson from that lifetime. Is it important for him to learn? Yes."

"I want you to lift him up into his higher self. That part of him that sees the lesson he has learned, is learning and has yet to learn."

Higher self? Are you available for communication? Yes."

"Please help him either silently or through his vocal cords. What lesson is he to learn from that lifetime?"

(I emit a series of soft sighs followed by a long pause. I begin to speak softly.)

"Shared knowledge. Shared money, shared health, shared feelings, shared thoughts, good thoughts for those around me. I don't have to know the people."

(Sobbing, I continue.)

"I never pick up coins on the ground. Leave them for someone else who needs it more."

"Okay," (Reassures Richard.)

(I continue, talking while still sobbing.)

"Take only what can be used. Ecology. Shared knowledge to make the environment better."

" Good," says Richard.

"Sounds like you got the lesson. Is that accurate, Subconscious Mind? I think so too," repeats Richard.

"Nathan, you can rest now. There is plenty of time for more work."

"Subconscious I want you to gently let him come back down to the conscious level."

"Subconscious Mind thank you for allowing me to work with you. Is there any objection to him coming back to an ordinary awareness at this time? No okay."

"I will count from one to five. As I count he will become more alert. At five he will open his eyes and be awake and alert, able to do what he has to do. Drive his car. Have a pleasant evening, a great sleep tonight and wake up refreshed and dynamic tomorrow."

"Subconscious Mind from your perspective, does he need any further work with the food allergies? No."

"I would encourage him to go slow with this. Yes."

"There will still be a shock to his system as he reintroduces these foods into his diet. Thank you again for allowing me to work with you."

"And now. One coming up, two coming up even more, three, breathing and heart rate coming back to normal, four almost at ordinary awareness, and five you are here with me and open your eyes."

Richard and I talked about the session for a few minutes. Again I was astounded by my awareness even though I was hypnotized. We discussed the fact that I had not shown any outward emotion at the revelation of the first experience with fermenting alcohol that went bad. Richard indicated my lack of emotion led him to the hypnotic suggestion of substituting love for fear in my DNA. As I reflect on this experience seven year later, and still gastritis free, I have become more aware of the power of suggestion to my mind and the human mind in general. I noted the words when he established the food allergies had been diffused throughout my body. The key to the success of relieving me of my food allergies and gastritis was the suggestion my subconscious replace all fear in my DNA with love, something it obviously did.

The key is the belief that it happened. Richard made the comment that is doesn't matter if you consciously believe in past lives or not. What counts is if the subconscious believes it. I knew the moment I saw Richard's work at the evening seminar that he could unlock the door to the cause of my gastritis. I was not disappointed.

During the final five days of our Florida vacation I did not consume any wheat. I continued to meditate each day to reinforce the continuing release of the negative energy that had been revealed during my single session with Richard. We returned to Memphis and I slowly began eating a slice of bread every other day. There was no reoccurrence of the usual gastritis.

For the next three months I focused on affirming the negative energy release by meditating and listening to the tape of my session with Richard. At the end of the first month I had experienced total relief from the gastritis that had plagued me for years. By the end of three months my mind and body had fully accepted that the negative source of the stress had been released.

During the next six to 12 months I would occasionally experience a gastric attack for some unknown reason. I would simply sit down and meditate for an hour, releasing the feeling and it would disappear. I had a gastritis attack one evening just before we were going to a party. I meditated for an hour and I was symptom free and enjoyed the food and drink in a normal fashion.

A Lesson Learned

There was more to be learned resulting from my first experience with Richard. The session had occurred at approximately 4 p.m. Part of the pent up negative energy was released emotionally and part of it was not. I had no idea how this energy was released and the power of these sessions, but I was soon to get my first glimpse of the mechanism and of its overall impact.

The next morning I played golf and my wife went shopping. She picked me up at the designated hour (3: 30 p.m.) and indicated she would like to make a couple of stops before we returned to the condo. I was very relaxed and in a good mood and readily agreed. As we were walking through one of the shops I suddenly got a very negative attitude and, without any apparent reason, Carroll Ann and I began to snap at each other. She indicated the shopping was over and we drove, in 20 minutes of dead silence, to the condo. Upon arriving she said she felt terribly nauseated and was going to lie down. Feeling just as badly, I went outside and set in a lounge chair on the beach, wondering what had just happened between us. The couple of hours apart seemed to calm things down, and the rest of the evening was a bit strained, but went without incident.

The next day we were driving in the area looking at real estate, something we routinely do when we travel. We were having trouble locating a particular subdivision and it was getting into mid afternoon. After we spent some time unsuccessfully scouting on our own my wife suggested that we stop at a real estate office I had passed several times and she would get directions. I was beginning to feel a bit anxious so I agreed and indicated I would stay in the car. She had been inside the office for just a few minutes when suddenly I began to have the same negative feelings I had experienced the previous day. I immediately knew that something was going on, but my wife was not with me, so I knew it had nothing to do with her. My stomach suddenly felt like I had swallowed a bowling ball and I felt very anxious. I looked at the clock on the car dash and saw that it was 4 p.m. It suddenly dawned on me. What I was experiencing now, and we had experienced the day before in the shop, was the same residual release of the negative emotional energy that my subconscious had started releasing during my session with Richard. It was the initial stage of my understanding that retained negative emotions, and therefore negative energies, are not necessarily released at one time, or immediately. Rather there is energy movement that can be random, or directed, and the duration of the release is directly proportional to the length of time it has been retained in our physical faculties, and the manner and intensity with which we release the emotions. My gastritis problem had been with me for almost 30 years.

The incident that took place the previous day had been a similar release. I calmed and centered myself for the next few minutes. Carroll Ann was fortunately detained in the building for at least 15 minutes, giving me ample time to acknowledge what was happening. (God is truly amazing when He orchestrates our experiences.) I calmed myself and allowed the negative energy movement to occur. It would be some eight years later before I would reduce this experience to the writing of a comprehensive theory.

When my wife came back to the car I related my experience to her. She confirmed my feelings by telling me, "all I knew was that yesterday while we were shopping I couldn't stand to be near you, and I couldn't understand why."

This was in January of 1994. It would take me years to fully experience and understand the implications of energy movement, but as the years passed, I came to recognize the inner energy actions that take place between persons is so powerful that it explains many of the personality conflicts we experience every day at home, on the streets, at work, and those between governing heads-of-state.

As I recall this episode I am strangely drawn to feel that in those few minutes I experienced the same release as depicted in the recent movie *The Green Mile,* when Big John, the mystic prisoner, releases the negative energy from his mouth in the form of small brown particles that fluttered upward and (symbolically) back to the universe.

In the following seven years I would be gently, and sometimes not so gently, exposed to the energy level exchanges that go on between humans, and between humans and the spiritual world. Most importantly the exposures led me to begin to recognize the processes that governs these exchanges and how to deal with them.

In the spring of 1999 on a week's skiing trip to Colorado, I met a young oriental woman who introduced me to the reality of absorbing other people's manifested negative energies. She taught me how to accept, and at the same time discharge, that negative energy before it settled into my subconscious and then manifested itself in my conscious being as pain.

In 1997 I experienced a summer-long obsession over a disagreement with a contractor, only to learn the spiritual world can, and often does, seize on an emotional weakness and leads us to dwell on occurrences that causes anxiety and pain. I learned how to release negative energies when dealing with spiritual entities. By the year 2000 I had come to experience and understand that I had been blessed with the Spiritual Gift of Mercy.

I found many times that when I was experiencing significant energy movements my wife would pick up on it and we would often have to sleep in separate rooms for a night to allow the energy to complete its movement, and/or dissipation, without negatively affecting her. This sensitivity is often referred to as feminine intuition, but it can be developed by both male and female, and is critical in manifesting the spiritual gifts, particularly those of healing and mercy.

Later I came to realize and understand that chronic absorption of someone's negative energy without release leads to discomfort, then pain, then physical disorders and ultimately, if intense enough, and not understood, and dealt with, premature disease and even death. Psychologists who deal with relationship problems (are there any other kind?) will often absorb these energies as they counsel their clients. The level of absorption will be proportional to the counselor's sensitivity and connectedness to the person they are counseling. If the release of this negative energy is not learned and exercised, they can develop joint and bone disorders such as arthritis, back pain, and other types of mobility disorders.

Early in my experience I read James Redfield's book, *The Celestine Prophesy* , that has an excellent chapter on personality traits and how they interact. It was the initial source of information that led me to my interest, study and theories on the awareness of the dynamics that occur between two or more interacting humans.

The results were, and still are, astonishing to me. So impressed were we with the results of my single session with Richard that my wife and I asked our daughter if she would like to see him during her spring break from graduate school. At this point she had been emotionally struggling to no avail, and she readily accepted the invitation. She and I would share one of the extraordinary experiences of our lives. It would be the beginning of her journey to reclaim her life that had been on hold for some 20 years.

CHAPTER 7
A FATHER'S LOVE

In mid March 1994 our daughter flew into Memphis from Colorado and the three of us continued on to Sarasota. Again we stayed on Long Boat Key, and Theresa had scheduled daily sessions with Richard. Her husband, Fred, would join us for a long weekend during our 10-day stay.

The year before, in Memphis, Theresa had several sessions with Jim Meade when Carroll Ann and I were present. Under hypnosis her subconscious related that she was carrying another entity. (In fact, more than one.) Jim got her to a certain point and could go no further. Theresa had several more sessions with Jim, but could never break through the blockage. Two weeks later, with no resolution, she and her husband packed up their U-Haul and headed west for graduate school in Colorado.

It was during one of these first sessions that I became aware of something that no one else seemed to recognize. As Jim probed and tried to expose the entity that was with Theresa, it showed its disdain for being disturbed and manifested itself by making snarling and curled lip remarks in responding to Jim's questioning as to who the entity was and why it was there. It was one of those moments that I have occasionally experienced, a knowing without realizing the full extent of what I know. Such was this case when I knew the entity with my daughter was evil in nature and would have to be dealt with. I had no idea how this awareness would try my soul, love, and sanity in the months to come.

Somewhere in the recesses of my mind, in that place somewhere between the conscious and the subconscious, I had retained the thought that my daughter was dealing with a negative entity that was influencing her life, and I was anxious to see if Richard would pick up on it. I had never said anything about this to either her or her mother for fear of influencing her sessions with Richard.

Once settled into our condo we would drive her into Richard's Sarasota office and wait for her session to be completed. Some days she would have two sessions, one in the morning and one in the afternoon. I had hoped to attend the session with her but she insisted on being alone. After each session I encouraged her to talk about their progress and she gladly shared them with us. On the first day, without making my intentions obvious, I questioned her on the possible presence of any entities in her aura. She indicated they had determined there were several entities present, but to my disappointment, Richard did not put much significance on their presence. He referred to them as "little gremlins." My heart sank. Deep within, my intuition told me there was a negative presence that had control over my daughter's life.

I went out to the beach for a long walk. I began talking to God, much as I had always done. Like most people, the intensity of my praying seems to raise when I need help and guidance. I walked for over an hour each day, telling God that I knew there was an evil presence that needed to be dealt with and to help us come to a fruitful conclusion on this trip. As I walked and talked with God I became totally engrossed in, and committed to, the concept of the expulsion of this entity. At some point I told God that I would do anything He wanted if He would take the entity from her. Even though I had been petrified during the period that I was enduring my own exorcism, I would take the entity onto myself if it meant freeing her from what she had been going through for the past 20 years.

As the days went by and the entities were ignored I became more convinced that if it were going to happen it would be through me. I began to envision my confrontation with the entity. I walked the beach and prayed continuously to God telling him that I was ready to do battle with this demon to free my daughter. I envisioned a session in Richard's office where he would help Theresa access her subconscious mind and I would then confront the demon head to head. The more I thought about it, the more I asked God to let it happen.

I remember on the fourth day I was returning from my walk when I had this undeniable urge to take off my tennis shoes and shirt and to wade out into the gulf waters. The implication here was significant to me. I enjoy being by the water, but I have an immense fear of being in water other than a bathtub or swimming pool where I can see the bottom. Without hesitation I started slowly but steadily walking out into the gulf. I had the feeling this was some sort of cleansing process. I walked out until the water was chest high. I never flinched, I never hesitated. Once to that point I simply turned around and returned to the beach and my clothes. I knew what would happen, I just didn't know how, or when.

As part of the plan our daughter's husband flew in for a long weekend. Things went well and we had a good visit. However, silently within me, my intense desire to take on this entity possessing my daughter grew by the hour. The feeling of love for her grew stronger and stronger, as did the disdain for the spiritual entity I knew I would face and the naive confidence I could deal with it.

We took Fred to the airport for his return trip home and it was under these most surprising circumstances that, literally, hell broke loose. At the airport Theresa took on a significant headache. We saw Fred onto his plane and then reached Richard on his pager and arranged to meet him at his office. The drive was approximately one hour. It was during this drive that I came to realize that God does not need a specific venue to perform His work. The vision I had of facing the entity during a hypnosis session between my daughter and Richard was purely in my imagination. At some moment the love I felt and the desire to free her from this demon was so strong, and at the time God so deemed it, He simply let it happen.

I knew it had happened because as I drove the car my intense feelings of love for my daughter abruptly turned to dislike and anger. I knew in those moments that I had literally absorbed the entity from her and that she was free of this negative force I had been focusing on. At the same time the feeling of anger and dislike was not from me, but was coming from the now-displaced demon. If the reader has trouble with accepting the reality of this occurrence, consider (Matthew 8:31-32), when Jesus indulges the entities and allows them to leave their hosts and move into the nearby herd of swine.

Theresa met with Richard while Carroll Ann and I waited outside his office. I said nothing about this to my wife. I really didn't know what to say. I just knew the entity was now with me. There was no fear this time. I knew that I had taken on this entity out of love for my daughter. No matter how unprepared I was to deal with such a transfer of energy, I was confident that God was with me.

Later that week we put our daughter on a plane for home, still unaware of what had taken place. Carroll Ann and I stayed at Long Boat Key for a couple of days and then went to Orlando and Disney World for two more days, and then home. The next three months would be equally as challenging and bizarre as any of the previous nine months.

On returning home I continued my daily meditation. In my inexperience I had felt that I had taken on the entity but I had no way of really knowing for sure. It was during meditations that it was affirmed that indeed I had asked God to free my daughter by my taking on the entity and my wish had been granted, my prayer answered.

Earlier I wrote about my hesitancy to channel outside spirits for the purpose of allowing them to use my physical faculties to transmit spiritual information to myself or others. I maintain that position, however, as you will note in my writings during the three months following my exorcism of our daughter's possession, I believe that true meditation can involve the channeling of one's own higher self. Thomas Keating writes of this in *Open Mind, Open Heart*. You may recognize the name of Edgar Cayce as the most noted channel of recent history. What is not well known about Cayce was that his mysticism started when he was a young child who had read the Bible from cover to cover by the age of 12.

In the book *The Story of Edgar Cayce* by Thomas Sugrue, Cayce is cited as discussing the difference between channeling other beings with profound information versus channeling, in his words, your Higher Self, or Christ Consciousness. He relates that channeling another entity is like trick shooting. It may be profound, but it does nothing for the channel's personal spiritual growth. He describes how to channel your higher self by going into meditation and focusing on your breathing only. Then focus on an ideal, not an idea. That, Cayce relates, is "being the best I can be." In my case, I focused on Jesus.

In Chapter 4, I alluded to a struggle for my mind. It was at this juncture the struggle ensued. As I researched my journal for details I found a revealing trend. In hindsight the struggle began shortly after our return from Sarasota in late March of '94 and continued for three months into the middle of May, but there is a perceptual change in the struggle. Early on, my being is accosted for the control of my heart, mind, body and soul.

As I researched my writings for this book, I became acutely aware of the value of journaling. Anyone who is struggling with physical, mental or spiritual problems will benefit from daily writing of your experiences and feelings. The writings may be of no immediate value, but months or years later when you review them, you may find as I did, a more objective and revealing truth of where you have been and perhaps where you are coming from.

It was only in the research and restudy of those journal notes that I came to appreciate the struggle between good and evil for control of my mind and, therefore, possibly for my very soul. The writings reveal the evolution of my spiritual condition during those three months. Note the feelings of anxiety and stress manifested in late March and early April of 1994 upon our return from Sarasota, then the inner resistance and strength shown as my commitment and dependency on God grew from the middle of April through late May.

Rather than reconstruct those weeks in today's words I find my feelings are better expressed using the actual dated journal entries in the chronology of their occurrence.

As a help in following the writings, I have included a brief glossary of words and terms that might be used by traditional religions and the metaphysical.

The Light or Spirit denotes God.

Brotherhood of White Light denotes the Angels of God.

Lower entity denotes Satan or demons.

Journal Entry - March 29, 1994 (Tuesday)

Monday afternoon and evening went well. I was tired but I felt very upbeat. Carroll Ann read the message I had received in meditation that indicated I had taken on the lower entity from Theresa and was upset. We went to bed around 10:30 p.m. I could not sleep and tossed and turned. I was nauseated. I kept getting words in my head, spelling the words. I seemed to want to get foreign words. One was "Vol-a-te". I do not know what that word means but suspect it is Spanish or Italian. I kept trying to get what I think was Italian or Spanish. I was getting energy surges too. Not uncomfortable but definitely energy. I continually spoke the name of God and Jesus. This went on for perhaps two hours. Finally around 12:45 a.m. my wife got up and had some warm milk and read. I said a rosary using my mother's beads. Around 1:15 a.m. she returned to bed and we both drifted off to sleep very easily.

I was awakened around 5:00 a.m. from a very negative dream, I would classify as a nightmare. I turned to my side and started to open my eyes when a vision appeared. It was a scrolling, repeating scene of what appeared to be some ancient or biblical signs and symbols. I get Egyptian. I do not remember seeing any words but I looked for them. The scrolling continued for some minutes. I just watched. Finally the scrolling stopped, but the picture remained in tact. Slowly, very slowly, it began to fade. Finally I opened my eyes completely and it disappeared.

My eyes had been partially open during the entire event. I suspect it lasted approximately five to six minutes. I am not surprised this happened because the previous morning I had been lying in bed next to my wife and I realized I was reading handwritten script on the ceiling with my eyes open. This occurred twice during a 15 minute period. When I became aware of it, of course it disappeared. I have no idea what the visions mean.

About the Dream

I do not remember the entire dream but I do recall the relevant parts. Early in the dream I was hanging around with a grade school classmate. I began to relate how he and two of his friends had always excluded me from their games. He asked if I wanted to know why and when I said yes, he reached over and slapped my face. This ended that part of the dream.

Later in the dream I was driving a car around a city and the streets were all in disrepair. The city maintenance crews were patching holes with blacktop. There was a tall and slender young man with me and someone else that did not seem relevant. The young man was very nice looking and he wore a black turtleneck and black trousers. He acted like he was a friend but I could tell he was not. He carried a walking stick that was stainless steel in color. It was tapered to a fine point at the tip. It looked like a large sewing needle, only the size of a sword or walking stick. He brandished it around, but not threateningly. At some point I became annoyed with his pretense to be my friend. I grabbed the end of the stick with my hands and began breaking the end into approximately 6 inch segments. The segments did not fall off. They were still attached to each other, but the instrument was now useless as a weapon. I broke perhaps the bottom one-third of the steel rod.

The dream then skipped to a scene where I was in a bedroom with my wife but we were in twin beds. She was asleep. I sat up in my bed and noticed the same young man had entered the room. He was still dressed in black and he carried no weapon or stick. He had a smile on his face, but I knew he was not concerned for my best interest. He began to take off his turtleneck. I had a small ice-pick like weapon that I began to thrust at him. He jumped back. I knew I penetrated him slightly but he still had a slight grin and look of surprise on his face. He did not show any sign of fear. At this point I woke up from the nightmare. I was frightened and then the vision I described before came to me.

For a long while after the vision disappeared I lay in bed wondering why God would send me such a terrifying dream right before this vision. I called on God and Jesus to be with me. I was discouraged and perplexed. I was not scared, just mystified. This went on for perhaps an hour and then I began to receive the following messages about the dream.

1. The first was about the grade school friend. My long time "friends" will turn away from me as my gifts unfold. This was symbolized by the slap in the face.

2. The young man in black represented lower entity(s) that I will come in contact with. They will appear as friends or they will be well camouflaged, but I will recognize them for what they are.

3. The stainless steel stick represented the power of the lower entities. My breaking the steel rod with my hands represents the power of God, or good over evil. The fact that the steel did not drop off when I broke it symbolizes that my power is limited to neutralizing, but not destroying them.

4. The final scene showing my wife and me in twin beds indicated that psychologically, and spiritually, I must learn to stand alone. The lower entities will continue to enter my life but I will recognize them. Again I do battle with them, but I cannot destroy them. There will be temptations with sexual overtones.

This is what I was led to understand the dream means. If this is supposed to be a gift, I am having a hard time being grateful. I can only say that I have a great feeling and need for the presence of God in me. I do not know how this will be used to help people, but I'm sure God does.

March 28, 1994 (Monday)

Today I had lunch with a young man who works for our company. He and I had talked about the reality of the spiritual world on several occasions.

I started telling him about the recent messages I had been getting while in meditation. As I was finishing I got a strong blocking signal that broke my speech and thought pattern. When this happens I know the person I am conversing with does not believe me. I asked him how he felt about my experiences and when he stammered I told him I knew he had rejected my thoughts. He agreed.

He asked me if I thought I was physically changing too. I laughed and related to him that in the past few days I had begun to look at myself differently in the mirror. At first I actually did double takes. My face looked younger. There is a definite difference in what I see in the mirror.

I began to tell him about how I felt the power to do these things was the power of God. Strangely as this point I began getting the same blocks. I was telling him the power was not mine but was coming to me from God. I dismissed the blocks at this point.

When I arrived home I decided to meditate on what had happened during the past couple of hours. When I meditate I concentrate on my breathing for about fifteen minutes and then I meet Jesus in my mind. Only this time I could not connect with Him. I did not feel right. I called on God to fill every cell of my body with the power of His light. I felt instinctively there was a lower entity blocking my connection with Jesus. When I called for the power of God over and over, and that only the presence of God could be with me, a tremendous surge of energy passed through my body again and again. My closed eyes were filled with the intensely bright, colors of fiery red and gold. I have never experienced brightness of such magnitude during meditation. It is my belief that this time the entity from my daughter's exorcism was expelled. I asked that it be taken away from me. I have since prayed to God that the entity be removed from our home.

March 30, 1994 (Wednesday)

I awoke this morning feeling very nervous and anxious. I went for a 15-minute walk. I feel a little better now, but not great. My temples feel pressure like I need to close my eyes.

I spoke to Jim Meade for the first time since the episode with my daughter in Sarasota. He agreed that I may have very well taken on the entity and that I should call on the Brotherhood of White Light to come and take the entity to the Light.

I went into a meditative state and acknowledged that I loved the entity as a creature of God. Not that I like it, but that I loved it as a creature of God. I asked the Brotherhood to take the entity from me. I pray the entity has been removed.

March 31, 1994 (Thursday)

I could not sleep Wednesday night. I said a rosary. Carroll Ann was having what appeared to be a restless dream. I lay and watched her for about 30 minutes, then got up and drank some warm milk.

I am still hearing the words "put the words down." This registered with me because I had no words to put down. Then the words from the energy book I am reading started running through my mind. "Sixth and seventh harmonics." I close my eyes and have an empty screen in my vision. The thoughts come.

"Harmonics will cause the oscillation of the magnetized material to become kinetic."

"It is as simple as it sounds. The trick will be to figure out what material. . . (silica iron) to use."

"The frequencies will not be difficult to come by. . . they are not audible."

"How will they be produced?" "That will come. It is available."

"There is much to do. That is all for now. Volate."

When I returned to bed I drifted off to sleep within five minutes. I awoke at 6:30 a.m. I am concerned about not getting enough sleep.

Later that same day I meditated again and got the following message.

"There is much to do. The music will stimulate the thoughts. You are free now. God loves you and has given you the privilege to deliver this gift to mankind. That is all for now. Salute."

"Is there any significance to the Italian words?" "No," was the answer I received.

April 1, 1994 (Friday)

I played golf today. I played terribly but enjoyed the outing. We went to bed about 10:30 p.m. and I could not go to sleep. Took a small amount of a tranquillizer but still could not fall asleep. There is an occasional light thump in my head just as I start to doze off. This went on for at least two hours. I finally drifted off to a restless sleep.

We awoke about 8:00 a.m. I had a very sexually oriented dream that involved friends of ours. I notice my thoughts have begun to return to a persistent sexual orientation. This sexual obsession has been absent for over 10 months. Under stress I think of sex because I know it is a stress release. Why has this suddenly returned to my thinking pattern?

April 2, 1994 (Saturday)

Saturday evening I am not tired. I get the message to "put it down on paper." So I enter a dialogue.

"Are you from the Light?" "Yes."

I go to the computer and I am asked, "what is it you want to know?"

"What will be the sequence of events?" "You must believe." Is the response I get.

"How do I do that?" "Place your faith in the Lord."

"I thought I had." "Your faith is weak right now."

"I know. I fear losing God. I fear the words are not from the Light. The words are weak. Did I get up to soon this time?" "No. Your mind is clouded."

"What can I do?" "Believe in the Word of God."

"What is the pulsing in my head?" "It is the opening of you mind to new ideas. You must approach this work with an honest mind. Do not deceive."

"Should I stop now?" "Yes."

"Will I sleep?" "No. The process is painful but we are of the Light."

April 3, 1994 (Sunday)

We went to bed about 11:30 p.m. and again I could not sleep. My eyes are flipping and flashing behind my eyelids with all types of patterns. I would almost doze off, then be awakened by this flashing. I asked if it were from the Light and I get no positive response. I get the urge to get up to write but I have made up my mind if I get no positive response I will not follow it. I am constantly praying and talking to God to take away any thoughts that are not of the Light. No sooner do I finish and start to drift off to sleep, but here comes these same thoughts. Is this a test? I don't like playing games with God.

The message in my mind is that there is no magnetic power source to be had. I will do other things. I find this very confusing and depressing. I doze off several times during the night only to reawaken. I am forced to sleep on my back. I always sleep on my side, but because of a slight but persistent chest pain I am on my back. No pain when I am on my back. I feel like I did not get very much sleep. It is depressing but I am less afraid than I have been in the past. I just don't like the confusion.

Why would I get a positive response to "are you of the Light" one night and nothing the next night?

April 4, 1994 (Monday)

During the entire day I have had this unbelievably strong urge to masturbate. I cannot understand this because there is no reason for it. Every idle moment seems to be filled with this thought. It is as if there is a test of wills going on. I don't even know if I believe masturbation is right or wrong, but one could not expect this kind of feeling to come from God. Therefore I feel I must be coming from a lower entity. I have resolved not to give in. There is no reason to. Is this some sort of test?

April 5, 1994 (Tuesday)

There were no dreams or problems last night. Today I started the medical preparation for my colonoscopy test tomorrow morning. There were no temptations. It is as if the battle is over.

April 6, 1994 (Wednesday)

The test went well and was negative. No sign of any reoccurrence of the polyp. I will repeat the test three years from now. Everything on the spiritual side is calm and quiet. No visions, no words, no head banging.

April 10, 1994 (Saturday)

My wife and I had perhaps the most intimate and honest conversation we have had in months. She indicated that she often gets this terrible feeling that she should not be around me. When she gets in bed she hopes that we will just go to sleep. She wants to talk to me but she gets this feeling of "don't talk to him." She often feels like she should leave.

She can't remember when it started, but it has become worse. She said she feels there is no reason for these feelings. Particularly towards me, but that something is driving her to feel this way. We discussed that perhaps meditation, which she does not do, would help control this feeling.

We also talked about attending church on a regular basis. Something we have drifted away from since her father passed away. Prior to her father dying she really enjoyed church but has recently lost interest.

We discussed that she could control the feelings by prayer and regular meditation. She will still have to fight the negative urges that will come until the Light fills her mind and spirit totally

April 15, 1994 (Friday)

Things are still quiet. It is as though the siege is over.

April 28, 1994 (Thursday)

Theresa called and is having all sorts of problems. She is having difficulty dealing with the changes she knows she will go through now that the entity is gone. She feels abandoned. I believe she is being pushed to find her true self now that she is free and there is understandably some fear in that.

I have noticed a very calm about my ability to handle daily crisis these past two weeks. Things just don't seem to bother or rattle me as they have in the past. Perhaps I am bored. I understand it is a natural reaction from not being constantly productive in a traditional work sense. I have started making some contacts outside my regular circle of friends and I believe some direction may come from these acquaintances.

May 1, 1994 (Sunday)

We went to church Saturday evening with my sister and her husband. Upon receiving communion Carroll Ann broke into tears. Later that evening she revealed to us they were tears of joy. That she had experienced an overwhelming feeling of joy when she received communion. Amen. The Light of God prevails.

May 4, 1994

I have decided that it would be a good idea to visit Jim Meade in Phoenix later this month to have him check out the presence or absence of the entity I exorcised from my daughter. We will make definite arrangements that will include a visit to the Grand Canyon.

I am sort of floating in the physical world. No big projects. No big problems. Physically I feel very good. Things are also very quiet on the spiritual side too. I am neither working, nor playing hard. I just seem to be stuck doing some non-mainstream projects. No stress to speak of. Maybe it's the quiet before the storm.

May 10 1994 (Tuesday)

I have meditated very little these past three weeks and my sex drive has returned to normal. Still interesting things seem to happen. I have been experiencing a period where I can ask God for something and I seem to get it almost instantly.

I can enter a situation that would normally put me into an agitated state, and I simply pray, "God put me in a relaxed and peaceful state," and suddenly all stress and agitation is gone. This reaction is not a perception. It is so obvious and immediate that I am easily aware that it is happening. It is a feeling of complete euphoric peace.

I have been practicing Reiki for the past three months. It is a hands-on healing ritual that uses symbols to activate healing powers within the body. The energy is dispensed through the hands that become elevated in temperature when practicing the symbols. I have now started using the same hands technique but I have found that I get even more energy and warming of my hands with the prayer, "God put me in a healing mode." My hands feel like a hot water bottle and are very relaxing to the recipient. I measured a temperature rise in my fingers of six degrees Fahrenheit.

The most enjoyable aspect of this unexpected gift is the effect it has on my golf game. For the past six or seven years I have scored in the mid 90s consistently. Rarely ever better. About fourteen days ago I played a round and using the admonition "God put me in a relaxed and concentrating mode" before each shot, and I shot a 90. Not really impressive but I could tell I was hitting better shots and I was not always focused on the words. Last Friday I played again and was well focused and used the same request before each shot. I scored an 80. I could have shot a 75 with a little more focus as I three putted 5 greens. An improvement of 15 strokes a round is a phenomenal improvement that cannot be explained in normal terms.

I have not asked for any special gifts and I suppose I will not. However I am thankful that I feel significantly better in my handling of daily emotions, or aggravations, by simply using the request "God put me in a letting go mode." It really works for me and I believe it will work for anyone who believes in the power of spiritual communication with God.

May 10, 1994 (Tuesday night)

I meditated using a headset and a tape entitled "Crystal Light Music." The tones sound like a melody of tuning forks and they resonate soothingly in my head. Making meditation and altered state easy to accomplish. I continued for about 15 minutes and was continually getting the purple mass in my mind's eye. I began to focus on Jesus. I found it to be fairly easy. After another 10 minutes I removed the headset and I am still focusing on Jesus and begin to write the first thoughts that come into my mind. Below is a list of the writings. Some of them are answers to specific questions.

"Pain is the way of life. It is the way of the Lord. It is the way of all mankind. It is the way to reach other people who are in pain."

"Have I ever given out of love of people?" "No. You give out of love of God."

"Should I give for love of person?" "Yes."

"What is the difference?" "Love of God is above love of man. Love of man expresses love of God at a lower level."

May 11, 1994 (Wednesday)

I enter meditation as described previously.

Purple mass is beautiful

Solitude (Answer to how I am feeling.)

"Beyond the One is many."

"The look of God is in you."

"You will write as often as you come to this place." (Office I leased specifically to write.)

"Subjects will come. Your intuition will give you subjects to write about."

"Yes. You will type easily in a meditative state."

"Purple mass is your third eye."

"You don't need 3rd degree Reiki. You already have the power to heal."

"You will remember what you have written."

"Jim Meade is good. See him often. Not for self, but you will help him relate to professionals."

I ended the meditation session and was very peaceful and content.

May 12, 1994 (Thursday afternoon)

Following same routine as the day before.

"Thought is the light."

"For all mankind you will do what is required of you to save mankind."

"Let no man put himself between himself and God."

"Religion is the foundation on which salvation is based."

"You are not afraid of the truth in meditation. Your subconscious mind tells you the truth."

"Be true to yourself. All else is sin."

May 16, 1994 (Monday)

I meditated to the Crystal Light Music.

"I am the light."

"The sun rises and sets on my Word."

"The Word is for all men of all races, of all beliefs."

"Ask and you shall receive, but you must be willing to receive."

"The Lord is with you in whatever you do."

"You must find your own path. You are on the right path."

"Why do men weep? They weep for themselves. The grace of God will dry all tears, eternity is man's destiny."

"Love is the answer you seek. It is the answer to your quest. Find it and you will be at peace."

"You have not found love of man, but love of self. Look outside yourself. Anywhere, everywhere."

May 17, 1994 (Tuesday)

"The light is here. Long live the light."

"The Word is the Light. Give to the world the power you behold."

"The sounds of trumpets will give you the answer."

"Beautiful is the Word and the Word is of God."

"Beauty is the beholder, for he is of God."

"The light is God and God is forever."

"Blessed are those who are of the light, for they shall see God."

"Men who have lived and died. Their bones will rise and be united. The flesh will be different. The spirit the same."

"To write, speaker of the truth, will take self discipline, sacrifice and patience."

"It was time to tell her. It is time for her to start dealing with her problems. (I have told my daughter about the exorcism I induced while we were in Sarasota.)

May 19, 1994 (Thursday)

"The entity from Theresa is with you. It is strong. It is what you asked God for. It will cause you much heartbreak. It cannot be removed except by penance. Theresa is free, or soon will be."

"You will not lose the love of God."

Note; The day after this I had a very strong session with my higher self and I asked God to take the entity to Himself. There was a very strong energy presence when I brought God to myself. I would be very surprised if the entity was not removed. However read the next entry.

May 23, 1994 (Monday)

"You don't come often enough. That is why you feel uncomfortable and unfulfilled."

"Yes the entity is still there, but you can control it with prayer and charity."

142

Note: I am concerned as to how the entity might manifest itself in me, or how it will try to manifest itself in me.

May 25, 1994 (Wednesday)

Writings during meditation.

"Behold the Lord is here."

"He stands among all men who ask.
The Lord comes to all who ask of Him."

"Blessed is the Lord."

"What does the entity want?" "Your soul."

"Will he get it?" "No, if you follow the Lord."

"What is its purpose?" "To create havoc, that is its only purpose."

"When did it come to Theresa?" "At her birth."

"The Lord will take the entity when you are ready to release it."

"You feel guilty about Theresa during her childhood. You should not."

"The entity is a figment of your mind."

"Love the Lord and love the entity. It cannot stand love."

"You are doing well."

"Love is not a temporal emotion. It is a way of life for the universe (patience). When the world loves, God is happy, darkness sad. Love will soon emerge in all people who survive the catastrophe."

"Your family is blessed."

"Do not fear, you have the love of God in you."

"Theresa is well too. She is free."

(End of Journal entries.)

———————————

As I relive those three months through my writings I am amazed at how my perspective on that time has clarified. It would appear that when I first returned from Sarasota the entity was trying powerfully to influence my spirituality towards an overt New Age manifestation. The sleepless nights, and the persistent urge to write during the night, the visions, the feeling of total frustration were all being influenced by the entity I had assumed from our daughter. It seems clear from my writings the objective was to use me as a channel. Yet through these early writings it is obvious that I am imploring God to be with me. I noticed that even though I have not consciously accepted the full reality of who Jesus is to me, I am asking for his presence in all of my meditations. He is the One I chose to be my guide and ideal.

The resulting stress and agitation during this time leads me to conclude the moving forces were lower entities. When we access their world we can become subject to the manipulations of the spiritual entities that reside there, be they good or evil. The spiritual world is not only comprised of angels and demons, but of spirits that are good, evil, and everything in between.

The turning point seems to come when I am besieged, but resist, the unusually obsessive sexual thoughts and inclinations, a problem I had not experienced since the exorcism of my lower entity in May of 1993. In the chronology of my writings this transformation seems to occur about April 5, 1994. One can venture speculation as to why it happened. Did God allow the early temptations to see how I would react? There is certainly biblical precedence in the book of Job for that belief. Another possible theory is that once the entity knew I was going to visit Jim Meade it changed its tactics and started to influence me in positive ways hoping that I would entertain its presence to preserve those powers.

My objection to the latter theory is that my prayers and intentions are all directed towards God. My thanks and appreciation for the good feelings is to God. There is no mention in my writings that I thought the powers were coming from some lower entity and that I considered retaining it. Further, in the Gospel of Matthew (12:25-26) Jesus relates. "And if Satan cast out Satan, he is divided against himself; how shall then his kingdom stand?" The limit to Satan's power is that he only promises us good, he can never deliver it. He can promise that if we follow a certain temptation we will experience pleasure and joy. However upon following that temptation, pleasure and joy are never experienced, but rather emptiness and guilt set in.

The meditations in the latter period seem much more Godly in nature. As I reflect on that period of time I now believe that I endured indeed, a struggle for my mind and soul. The early period is definitely the influence of lower entity(s). I am not sure what caused the transition, but I believe that the latter part of the period is the influence of God. Perhaps God wanted to see how I would react to the challenge of the sexual temptations. Perhaps He wanted me to experience the powers, and the visions that go along with humans engaging the spiritual world.

Personally, I feel that once I resisted the temptations to follow the early inclinations, God instilled his blessings on me in response to my continual prayer and call for his presence and protection. If one can express the feeling of experiencing "Heaven on Earth." it would be the blessings and feelings of euphoria and control over my daily emotions that I had in those final weeks of May 1994, by simply calling on God's help with the admonition, "God put me in a letting go mode." I had never experienced that level of serenity before and I would not experience it again until the summer of 2002.

Once I knew I had transferred the entity to myself, I never was seriously tempted to retain it. I was frustrated that I could not expel it myself, something I did not learn to do until the summer of 1997. I also never felt threatened by its presence and I felt safe in the love of God because God knew that I took on the demons for the purpose of freeing my daughter. I believe the protection was God's way of rewarding me for the act of selflessness, albeit in hindsight I was foolish to do it without the proper spiritual preparation.

I have come to understand that man learns spiritual lessons both from the good and the evil of the spiritual world. If I have an encounter with an evil spirit against my intentions, do I have faith that God and His angels will protect and deliver me? Is this not an extension of the faith we read about in the Gospels? Jesus goes out into the desert for 40 days to fast and pray. The Gospels tell us that He had an encounter with Satan. Not only a passive encounter, but an extended one that involved His purposely engaging Satan to test His commitment to God's Will. Are we to be afraid that if we are seeking God in our spiritual journey and we encounter evil that God will not deliver us? This is a theological question I cannot answer for anyone but myself. God has seen fit to allow me to walk on what I have perceived as the spiritual precipice and each time I return I feel more connected and subjugated to God's Will and more at peace with my life.

I cannot say for sure why the sequence of events happened, just as I cannot say why many of my experiences happened. Perhaps they happened so that one day I would share them. One thing it should not do is frighten anyone from meditation. True contemplative prayer with a focus on God made me a better spiritual person and brought me closer to God because that was my sole intention. We are aware that strife and temptation make us stronger when we surface from them in the Light of God. .

It was now time to finally deal with the entity(s) that I exorcised from our daughter and set the stage for my further spiritual growth. That growth would include a developing intuition, and guiding awareness of the Holy Spirit's presence in me, while in contact with persons having emotional pain.

CHAPTER 8
FREE AT LAST, FREE AT LAST

Upon returning from Sarasota in late March 1994 I discovered the entity that had been with my daughter since her birth was now with me. From the previous chapter's readings the reader can infer that I continually felt I had successfully exorcised the entity from myself, only to find failure. It would be several years later before I would discover the power, available to all of us, to deal with demonic powers. At some point I knew that if its presence persisted I would visit Jim Meade and ask him to help me remove it.

I made contact with Jim in April and as time went by it became obvious to me I would need his help. We finally made definite plans and on May 27, 1994, my wife and I flew to Phoenix to visit him. We stayed at a local motel and the next day we drove to his home, where we spent the morning and lunch visiting with Jim and his wife. After lunch, Jim suggested that he and I retire to his study and talk about the problem at hand.

The previous chapter gives the reader sufficient background needed to move into this episode. I can only say that I was not prepared for what happened next. Below is a transcript of our session on May 28, 1994, ironically, it was exactly one year to the day from my daughter's first session with Jim, when the entities first revealed themselves to me. Something I was unaware of until I began the research for this book.

Entity Transcript

Jim starts with the same melodic, deep and soothing voice that is his trademark. He takes me through the stages of hypnosis and then, when I am completely relaxed, begins to address my subconscious mind.

"I want to speak with Nathan's subconscious mind. Subconscious mind, once again I want you to feel the joy the peace and happiness associated with the word yes. In a few moments I am going to ask you to cause one of his fingers to move to indicate the word yes." (Pause.)

"Now once again Nathan, you may or may not be aware that the fingers are moving or even attempting to move. But I do not want you to concern yourself with this. Allow your conscious mind to go to a different time, to a different place, even to a fantasy of its own choice, and to remain there until I call it back."

"Once again subconscious, I want you to feel the joy, peace and happiness associated with the word yes, and

I now want you to cause one of his fingers to move indicating to me the word yes, and to do that now."

(Pause. Then my right index finger rises off the chair.)

"All right I understand. You may relax that finger."

"Subconscious, I now want you to cause a different finger to move indicating to me the word no, and to do that now."

(My little finger rises off the chair.)

"I understand."

"Subconscious mind, each and every breath will take him deeper, much deeper as he lets go and steps aside, much deeper. Once again subconscious you are the one who guides and protects Nathan. Is this true? Yes, all right."

"And you are the one who has recorded his experiences in the present life time, or any previous life times? Yes, all right."

"Subconscious mind I need your help today. I need your help to work with Nathan. Are you available to do that? Do you understand? Yes, all right."

"The first thing I want you to do." (Pause.) *"Subconscious mind is to examine his aura. I want you to examine his aura from head to toe. Front to back, from side to side. Is there someone within his aura subconscious?"* (Pause.)

"Is there a spirit within the aura? Yes, there is."

"Is there more than one? Yes, there is more than one?"

"Are there more than five within his aura? Yes, there is."

"Are there more than 10 within the aura? There is."

"Are there more than 15? No."

"Are there more than thirteen in his aura? No. All right."

"Are there 12 and 12 only? Yes, there are 12 within the aura. I understand. You may relax now."

"Subconscious mind, the ones who are there in his aura. They came to him since we last worked? Yes, all right."

"Is that because he consciously drew them to him? Yes, it is. All right."

"Are these the ones who were attached to his daughter? They were. All right."

"Would they like to communicate with me? Yes, all right, you may all use his vocal cords and speak to me."

"What is it you are trying to accomplish with Nathan?"

(I groan aloud and stir in my chair. Guttural sounds. Humnn. Adum, agumm. I begin speaking in a voice with a tone and texture that I have never heard before. It is my voice, but it is a least two octaves lower than my normal tone and staccato in rhythm. On tape it sounds ominous.)

"I'm the devil." (These are the first words out of my mouth.)

(Jim replies.) *"No, there is no devil,"* (I sigh.)

(Jim continues in a voice that indicates he is telepathically communicating directly with these entities.) *"The devil only exists in the mind of man. You work through fear."* (Pause.)

"Yes I know you do."

(Jim asks the entities inquisitively.) *"Why not join us in the light? Join us in love. Wouldn't you prefer that?"*

"The light blinds me." (Replies the entities continuing to use my voice.)

(Jim responds.) *"The light does not need to blind you."*

(The entities persists.) *"But it does."*

(Jim continues.) *"But it can be brought to you in loving levels, in steps. The light is love. Love is what blinds you."*

"I was happy where I was." (The entities continue.)

(Jim asks.) *"With Theresa?"*

(Entities.) "Yes."

(Jim presses on.) *"Where did she pick you up, in Colorado?"*

(Entities.) *"At her birth."*

(Jim replies.) *"All right."*

(On the tape I can hear the deep breaths I am taking.)

(The entities volunteer.) *"There was trauma in her birth. She almost died. The trauma opened up her aura for us to enter."* (Pause.)

(The entities repeat.) *"We were happy there."*

"At the time of the birth." (Pause.) *"The aura was weak at that time. She almost died and we stepped in to take over the body."*

(Jim continues the thought.) *"Rather than have one of your own, you wanted to capture one?"*

(The entities reply.) *"Yes."*

(Jim responds.) *"All right."*

(There is a deep breath.)

(The entities volunteer.) *"She is free."*

(Jim replies.) *"All right."*

(The entity continues.) *"This foolish one thought he could deal with us."*

(Jim patiently replies.) *"Right."*

155

(The entities relate to Jim.) *"He may be surprised. You may be surprised."*

(Jim questions the entities.) *"I may be surprised?"*

(The entities repeat.) *"You may be surprised."*

(Jim questions the entity.) *"Why would I be surprised?"*

(There is a long pause and no response from the entity.)

(Jim continues to speak to the entities.) *"I have requested the brotherhood of the White Light to join me. Is that what you want?"*

"No." (The reply is quick and seemingly intimidated.)

(Jim questions the entities.) *"I have dealt with others that have been controlling through fear. Do you understand that?"*

"Yes, but it is this ones choice to let us go. He brought us to himself." (States the entity.)

(I feel in listening to the tape that the entities feel the only way they can be forced to leave is if I choose to let them go.)

"Do you wish for me to bring in the Brotherhood of White Light?"

(Long pause. and sigh. The entity speaks through me.)

"Could we go. . . somewhere, where we will not be bothered?"

(Jim asks.) *"Where would you like to go?"*

"Home." (Is the short reply.)

(Jim states.) *"That is to the light. That is where you originally came out of love."* (Pause.)

(Jim continues to the entities.) *"The God that originally created you, created you out of love, and you turned your back on that love."* (Pause.) *"But that love has never been turned away from you."*

"Wherever home is." (Is the reply of seeming resignation.)

(Jim continues.) *"You would like to return back there?"*

"Yes." (Is the reply.)

(Jim asks.) *"All right. Is there anything else I need to know?"*

(There is a long pause.)

"This one is not as strong as he thought." *"Yes."* (Agrees Jim.)

(Again there is a lengthy pause.)

(Jim repeats.) *"Are all of you ready to go now?"*

"Yes." (Comes the quiet reply.)

(Jim continues.) *"All right."*

(Suddenly I am speaking on my own to Jim.) *"No, No."*

(Jim asks me.) *"What is it Nathan?"*

(Another long pause as I am apparently trying to discern what I am feeling.)

"There is not a true desire to leave. I don't think they are telling you the truth. Hua ha". (I hear myself chuckling.)

(Jim demands.) *"Do all of you want me to force you out? That will be your choice."* (Continues Jim.)

(I continue to give Jim my inner feelings.)

"They don't think you have the power?" (I relate to Jim.)

(Jim responds.) *"Okay."*

(I continue to verbalize my inner feelings.) *"I don't think they are convinced that I want them to go either."*

(Now I speak with conviction and firmness.) *"But I do. They serve no purpose. I do. . . I do. I want only the presence of God, the presence of the Light. I want to be free of these entities."*

(Jim states authoritatively.) *"Then thy will be done."*

(There is a sudden rush and feeling within me and I omit a verbal "whew," as I feel my breath being taken away.)

"So be it now." (As Jim senses that my conviction is true and fruitful.)

(I take a deep breath and there is a long pause. I sniffle.)

(Jim continues.) *"The God within you has so directed and so ordered You brought them to yourself and you have the power to expel them. That is how much power lies within you."*

(I begin sobbing with joy.)

(Jim speaks to me with conviction.) "The Living God lies within you."

(There is silence and a long pause and now I am breathing slower.)

(Jim asks.) *"Are the rest of them ready to go now?"*

"Subconscious, I am going to gently touch Nathan on the hand and I want them to feel this energy of love."

(Jim continues.)

"There is no reason to be afraid. No fear. But I can change that energy. The God that lies within me can direct that energy in a different way. Now."

(Sigh and long pause.)

(Jim asks.) "Subconscious mind, did they like the second energy? No, it can be intensified ten thousand times if that's what they want. But I don't want that."

*(*I ask out loud). *"Do we know if they are still here?"*

(Jim speaks.) *"Nathan let go and go deeper. Deeper, down, letting go and melting down. Melting down. Letting go. I call on the brotherhood of white light to guide them out. Take them out of the room. No harm is come to them my brothers. No harm is to come. Bring them into the light but slowly. We do not wish to have them destroyed."* (Pause.)

"Once again subconscious I want you to examine the aura. Is the aura now completely clear? Yes. All right." (I am breathing deeply.)

"All right now. I want you to visualize a beautiful rainbow coming out of a white cloud. Let the creative energy of that rainbow descend down upon you now." (Pause.)

"You are now completely surrounded by this energy. Now I am going to count to five and as I count, feel yourself being lifted up into that rainbow moving to the highest reaches of your own mind. Where you will find yourself at the top of your own mind. Being there, in that higher self, that Christ conscious mind."

*"Number one feeling yourself being lifted up now.
Number two, feeling yourself being lifted up even more
into your own mind. Number three, moving up even
more. Feeling yourself drifting up even more. Four,
you are almost there, and number five passing into that
beautiful white cloud and now coming out on top."*

(Long pause.)

(I mumble anxiously.)

(Jim questions me.) *"What is it?"*

(I reply.) *"Jesus is not here."*

(Jim states.) *"Someone is there with you."*

(I continue.) *"I don't want to look at him."*

(Jim questions me.) *"You don't want to look at the one
who is there?"*

(I affirm.) *"Yes."*

(Jim asks me.) *"Why?"*

(Pause.)

(I reply anxiously.) *"It wasn't Jesus. It was not good. It was different."*

(Jim continues.) *"There is no good and there is no bad. There only is what is. Fear brings you to that position. Look at that one with love. Totally with love, and watch the continence change."*

(Very Long Pause. Sigh and deep breathing.)

(Jim asks.) *"Is the countenance of that one changing?"*

(Pause. Then I reply.)

"No but I am . . . . . .I am not afraid. It is darkness, a black."

(Jim interjects.) *"The one that stands before you represents fear, that is all."*

(I affirm his comment.) *"Yes I know that."*

(Jim continues.) *"Christ stands beside you. You do not see Him yet. He wants you to look at this."* (Pause.) *"To focus on that darkness and turn it into light. To let go of the fear. If that is what God wants then that is what will be."*

(Jim asks me.) *"Is that what you want Nathan?"*

(Without hesitation I reply.) *"Yes."*

(Jim questions me.) *"Do you want what the God within you wants?"*

"Yes, I want what the God within me wants."

(Jim responds.) *"Then so be it now."*

(Pause, and then I speak in a slow but assured tone.) *"Yes, yes.. . . . Yes, yes."*

"You have the power. It comes through you from God, the God that lies within you. Do you understand that Nathan?"

"Yes." (Deep breath.) *"Jesus, yes."* (I moan.) *"Jesus is with me now."*

(Jim responds.) *"Yes, He has always been with you. He is your teacher."* (Long pause.)

"I have much to learn." (I verbalize.)

(Jim assures me.) *"You have much to unfold, that's all. There is much knowledge for you to open up to. It is there within you now."*

"Yes I believe it is within me. Yes." (Long pause.)

(At this point I seem to be getting some inner message that is not unusual during these sessions.)

"I believe that the power to unfold comes from without. The unfolding is from within. Once I am totally in touch with the God light. Once I eliminate the fear. I believe that God has put within me the power to do what ever is good. Love is the answer." (As I complete the thought.)

(Jim agrees.) "That's right. There are only two things, love and fear. So let go of the fear. Let that creative love work through you. The creator enjoys his creations through the creative, and the creative enjoy the creator through his creations."

(I continue my thoughts.) *"The steps of evolution, the steps of evolvement often require help from outside, a facilitator. We need each other. Lest all men would love all men and there would be no war. And there would be no sorrow, and there would be no sadness, and there would be no darkness. But until that time, when all men are open, they must seek help from a higher plane until they themselves can trigger the transformation of themselves. Man's mind is both his biggest asset and his biggest liability."*

(Jim interjects.) *"That is where free will comes in."*

"Yes, that's what separates us from the rest of creation." (I reply. Pause and continue.)

"The light is the salvation of man until all men, or most men, know only love. Until that time, man depends on the light to help elevate him to his inner goodness."

(Long pause.)

(Jim speaks to me.) *"Okay. Nathan, just feel the healing energy moving into you now."* (Long pause.)

"Subconscious mind is it time to bring him back to full awareness? Yes, all right."

Jim begins the process to bring me back to full awareness.

"Once again I am going to count from one to five and you will be back with me. Number one, coming up you are at peace with yourself and the world and everyone in it. Number two coming up even more with a sense of joy and happiness. Knowing once again your aura is cleared and sealed. The Brotherhood has sealed it once again. Number three coming up even more. Number four coming up, and number five eyes open and back with me.

(My voice perceptually changes in animation and raises one or two octaves.)

(I speak jokingly to Jim.) *"That was your second best work, the first time being your best."*

(Jim reviews the moment of truth with great enthusiasm.)

"When you made the statement I want this, I want them cleared, and I said 'thy will be done.' Wham. They were gone, that was it."

(I agreed.) *"Yea, I could feel it. It took my breath away."*

"I knew that I was not yet at the confidence level to move them out on my own. It was very intense. God it was so intense." (I conclude with almost a whisper to myself.)

(I continued to explain.) *"Whew! They were shutting down Theresa so I had to bring them out. The only thing I could think of doing was to bring them to myself. Then I couldn't seem to release them on my own. Now they are gone from both of us."*

(Jim agreed with a tone of empathy.) "Yes. It worked out for both of you."

NOTE: In these first 12 months I had come to know people who believed that God was completely with, and indivisible from, the human spirit. These encounters would change forever my understanding of the meaning of omnipresence. Previously I thought it meant God "could be" anywhere He wanted to be. It is one thing to intellectually know of God's omnipresence, it is something else to experience and feel His actual presence with, and within, my physical senses.

Summary

Unlike my first episode with an entity, I was never frightened by this encounter. I had stayed tethered closely to God and I always felt He would protect me. As I look back on this experience and the many that were to follow, I believe that God was always there, always monitoring my encounters, allowing them to go far enough for the lessons to be learned. I had again experienced the reality of the spiritual world and found a way to express the love for my daughter that had been suppressed during her childhood because of the influence of my first spiritual attachment.

As I review the transcripts in the summer of 2001 it would be easy to point out the differences in my theology today from seven years ago. Yet good comes in many packages. In (Mark 9:38-40) Jesus speaks to his apostles who return to Him telling Him they have rebuked those who were casting out devils in His name because they were not part of their inner group. Jesus explains to them, "those who are not against us are with us."

In the spiritual world there are many roads to the truth. I have come to understand that experiencing the spiritual world and its benefits and dangers, and salvation, are two distinctly different experiences. People can, and do, access the spiritual world everyday with no intention of furthering their road to salvation. Accessing the spiritual world for other than salvation does not automatically mean a person is embracing Satan. The spiritual world can be, and has been, the source of many great gifts of music, art, science and life enhancing information. The problem is knowing if what you are receiving is the truth, and from God.

The source of global ethnic cleansing is almost always religious based. It begins with misunderstandings and eventually escalates to pure and simple dislike, and then hatred. Yet all of these misunderstandings are based on a belief that "my" religion is better, or more correct than yours.

Man often confuses salvation with spirituality. We all recognize good can come from someone who does not share our religious persuasion. Buddhists regularly access the spiritual world. Some Christians do not believe that a Buddhist is saved. Does that mean the Buddhist is accessing Satan? Hardly. If you read of revelations received by Buddhist monks in meditation you could hardly differentiate them from those experienced by Teresa of Avila, Therese of Lisieux and John of the Cross. All three are highly revered saints of the Catholic Church.

As you follow my story you will notice that God sends me lessons in the form of people of all cultural and religious persuasions, just as you find He sent to Jesus in the last three years of His ministry. We never learn without teaching and we never teach without learning. There are several passages in the Gospels that illustrate lessons learned when Jesus encounters those previously considered unacceptable by His Jewish traditions. Some of these are the story of the centurion in (Matthew (8:10-13); the gentiles in Matthew (10: 5-6.); the woman begging for crumbs from the table in Matthew (15:24-28); and the Samarian woman in John (4:7-24).

As we left Jim's home and continued on our trip to the Grand Canyon, Carroll Ann and I stopped in Sedona, Arizona, known for its energy vortexes, and then went on to the north rim of the Grand Canyon. The Canyon is an awesome sight and manifestation of God's power.

I played the tape of my session for my wife in the car. I remember the awareness I had of the texture and tone of my voice. It was the same awareness I had when I first witnessed the entities, then again with my daughter, responding to Jim's questions. The voice (my voice) on the audiotape was ominous. Never before or since has my voice had such a negative quality to it.

To say I was dumbfounded by what was revealed would be an understatement. I had known I had absorbed an entity from my daughter, but was not prepared to hear there were 12 of them.

My wife and I had a pleasant visit at the Grand Canyon, then returned home for two days and traveled on to Destin, Florida, for a week with our son and his family. By the end of that two weeks period all of the unique powers that I had manifested for the previous six weeks, described in Chapter 7, would vanish. It would be many years later and under entirely different circumstances, before I experienced such euphoria again. However, I was thankful to be myself again. I was free, free at last.

NOTE; today is July 4, 2001. I arose early this morning to review and edit Chapters 5 through 7 of this book. As I read Chapters 6 and 7 and the rather mind-boggling meditations I wrote, doubts came into my mind concerning the source of all that I have experienced. I took a break and closed my eyes in brief meditation. I then opened my *Daily Devotional* booklet and found the following writing for today's thought.

Walking With Hagar

"So Hagar put the child down under a shrub, and then went and sat down opposite him." Genesis 21:15-16

"I have puzzled over the account of Abraham's family for many years, but now when I read it, I spend some time with Hagar, the Egyptian who bore Abraham's son Ishmael and later was sent out into the wilderness. I sit with her as she waits, a bowshot away from her child Ishmael so she will not see him die of hunger. She loves her son but cannot look at his suffering. We wait together, Hagar and I, not knowing how God intends to bring good out of evil.

My small pains and disappointments become smaller as I recall how this woman has obeyed Abraham's directions and set out with only a skin of water, some bread and her son. What was ahead of her except lost dreams and then death? We sit together, Hagar and I, until Ishmael's cry to God gives Hagar new life. God's messenger tells her to take Ishmael's hand and to walk a little further. I watch Hagar go to her son. I see them walk a little farther. God is with them.

Can I stand now, walk a little farther, and hear God speaking in what happens and has happened to me?"

Sr. Marguerite Zralek, O.P.

One cannot live with an open mind and not hear, feel and see the infinite goodness of God in all that is, the living God who knows exactly what we need and when we need it. Yes, I can walk a little farther to see where this book will take me.

CHAPTER 9
FINDING JESUS, AGAIN

There was often more than one scenario unfolding simultaneously in my spiritual evolution. The period between November 1993 and all of 1994 was no exception. I now take the reader back to November 1993 for a look at a second series of experiences that unfolded simultaneously with those described in the previous four chapters.

In November 1993 the name Jesus Christ began its uninvited entrance into my mind, and my perceived relationship with God was being affected by its persistence. To complete this story I need to relate other relevant happenings that occurred during this time.

In late November or early December of 1993 I was very attuned to God and to the spiritual world. I was very much into meditation and my life was spent contemplating and praying to God. It was during this time that for no apparent reason the name Jesus Christ began popping into my thoughts. It was rather disturbing. I had established a good one-on-one communication with God and I was afraid that changing my mode of operation might very well tick off

God. I made a special effort to subdue these unsolicited thoughts about this Jesus Christ. The thoughts coming to me were to pray to Jesus or to include him in my talking with God. I was very anxious about this and very concerned that it was disrupting my relationship with God. These thoughts continued to arise into the next year.

While I was trying to figure out who, what, and why the name Jesus Christ was coming into my thoughts, my wife told me one day in November that, without provocation, she began to have a panic attack about losing touch with Joel and Lee Jennings, a couple we had met in 1963, in Wheaton, Illinois. We lived next to them for about 15 months in side-by-side six flats. We had moved to Park Forest in 1964, and we had maintained a once or twice-a-year visit with the Jennings, who eventually had four children. The last time we had seen them had been 1975 in Minneapolis. We had visited them at their home and thought they were still very much the same as they had been. We enjoyed the brief visit, but we had had no contact with them since 1975.

I can tell you my wife is like a bird dog, when she gets the scent there is no stopping her. Though it had been over a quarter of a century, she tracked and found Joel and Lee located in a Minneapolis suburb. She spoke with Lee briefly and they talked about getting together in the summer of 1994.

The day after Christmas, 1993, we left for Long Boat Key, Florida, where we were now spending four or five weeks each January. As we were leaving Memphis, I called Joel and we had an engaging hour-long conversation. I told him he could count on us visiting them the coming August at their lake house on Gull Lake. Having made that reconnection we were off for what we thought was just more fun in the sun.

I have already described how finding Dr. Richard Schulman in the bookstore window affected my life. The other person it was suggested that I see while we were in Sarasota was Mary Park. Mary had her unique place in my spiritual journey.

I had Mary Park's name and number, but I had not called her and was not moved to do so, when one night I heard my name being called aloud in my sleep. I woke up with a start and sat upright in the bed and a very pronounced presence told me to call Mary. The next day I did and, through a series of rather strange happenings on her end, she was unexpectedly home and could see me. We drove about 48 miles to visit her. She was a pleasant, slim brunette in her 40s. She was known as a mystic who did readings for people. Her most significant undertaking was the drawings that were spiritually communicated (channeled) to her. She would work on them in spurts. These activities were always at night. She painted the most beautiful angelic and heavenly scenes. The uniqueness was that her drawings were actually in some unknown script. Every line or marking on the large drawings, which were very intricate, were composed of this script. My sister Mary is an artist and she said it would take her probably two or three days just to set up one of these paintings. Mary Park did a complete drawing every night. She would do seven or eight in a row, one drawing each night.

As we sat in her breakfast room table she spoke to us. She explained that she did not go into an altered state to give a reading. The information just came to her. She was the first person, although not the last, to tell me I was a "star person." She said all she saw as she looked at me was a bright light. Apparently the overly bright aura indicates a star person. She told me I had a very strong energy presence and she intuited my gastric problems. She told me that until I learned to "give of myself" I would continue to suffer with this problem. I resisted what she was saying, though not verbally. We continued talking for a while and she then asked me "why do you resist me when you know what I am saying is true?" Somehow I knew that she was right. I had given money in support of inner city ministries, but my work had prevented me from getting involved with these ministries in a hands-on way. Later in the meeting she told me I should study Reiki, which is a form of hands-on healing. Before we left she offered to do a "hand print" for each of us. She traced our hand with a pencil onto a blank piece of white paper and after our departure she filled it in with script and pictures and mailed it to us. We spoke on the phone for about an hour and she explained what she had been given. Both Carroll Ann and I were to be significantly surprised.

It is important for the reader to understand there were two scenarios playing out simultaneously in late January 1994. When I decided to write about my experiences I wrestled with how to separate them and in what order they should be presented. All of the encounters are interwoven but the encounter with Mary led to several spiritual experiences that unfolded during the remainder of 1994. It should be sufficient that the reader understands this story is unfolding in the same time frame as my first session with Dr. Richard Schulman. The time frame was January through March of 1994.

We returned home from Sarasota in early February. I began looking for someone who practiced the healing art of Reiki. Following Mary's advice I had decided that I would pursue Reiki as a means to learn to give of myself, but I wanted to experience it before I studied it. I called a local homeopathic doctor, who led me to a young lady by the name of Betty. Betty called, and she came to our home a week later. She brought a massage table and worked on me in our spa room.

Reiki is an ancient form of hands on healing that involves focusing healing energy into the hands, causing the temperature of the hands to rise significantly. The generated energy is then transmitted to the patient by either actually touching the patient or holding the hands slightly above the patient's body. The energy is generated by mentally repeating the drawing of symbols. The Christian world would undoubtedly refer to using the symbols as "paganistic," however it does work. In Christian healing services the practitioner calls on The Holy Spirit to infuse Himself into the hands, and subsequently into the patient. I first studied and practiced Reiki and later learned the same healing results could be obtained by simply calling on God to "put me in a healing mode."

The session with Betty was a pleasant enough experience. It lasted about 30 minutes and afterwards, being gifted with visualization, she told me that she saw many healing animals surrounding me. She saw me as a shaman (a native Indian healer). She also told me the one thing I knew was true. I was allergic to oranges. She told me my shoulder problem was because of a strained family relationship. There was no way she could have known about these last two realities.

She returned a second time and said she was told not to tell me any more, that it was time for me to pursue the inner knowledge for myself. The third time she came she said even less. She finished the healing session and I sat on the couch while she sat, crossed legged, on the floor in front of me, her head down and eyes closed. I immediately asked her, "What did you see?" After a pause she slowly and quietly said "I saw Jesus Christ on the cross." Immediately I was transfixed. I was still having the name Jesus Christ pop into my head and was now kicking it out just as quickly as it occurred. I leaned forward and looked down at her. Her head was still bowed. "What do you think that means?" I asked inquisitively. To the day I die I will never forget her response. She slowly raised her head, opened her eyes, looked at me and quietly said, "I don't know, I'm Jewish." I abruptly sat back in the couch, my eyes glazed in realization. After five months of having the name Jesus Christ come into my thoughts, this young Jewish girl was now leading me to take the next step. Betty never came back, although I was to meet her again as part of the Reiki class I would take later that spring.

Coincidences? The name of Mary from Jim Meade the previous fall. The name of Jesus Christ coming into my thoughts. The calling of my name while I slept in Sarasota, and the urgency to call Mary. The unexpected timing of her availability and our getting together. Her intuiting of my gastritis and the recommendation to studying Reiki. All leading to a young Jewish girl telling me that she saw Jesus Christ on the cross in the energy surrounding me.

Coincidences? Perhaps some may think so, but of course I knew what it meant. I needed to find out once and for all: Who was this Jesus Christ?

So began my quest to find out about Jesus. You may already have guessed that truth is stranger than fiction, and I began looking in all of my metaphysical sources.

I did find some writings by mystics who had ideas and thoughts about Jesus as a prophet and great teacher. The answer I was seeking would not come easily, or quickly.

CHAPTER 10
THE WORD AND THE
FEATHER

The spring of 1994 ended and another long hot summer came to Memphis. My quest was not yet answered, and the name Jesus Christ was even more persistent in my thoughts. Now I was urgently trying to figure out who he was.

August came and we flew to Minnesota to visit the Jenningses, whom we had not seen in 25 years. They picked us up in two cars. The spiritual conversation started as soon as I got in the car with Joel. As much as I was steeped in the metaphysical, I was to learn, The Scriptures were just as engrained in Joel.

They asked us to stay at their home Saturday night and attend church (Evangelical) with them Sunday morning.

The next morning we attended church together. There was a "Big Church" service with inspirational singing and an even more inspirational spiritual talk by a young lady. We then went to "Small Church," where Joel was to conduct Bible class. The Small Church lasted about an hour. The gathering opened with a prayer and a lot of discussion about who was sick, who needed help, who was in the hospital and who needed prayers. This was all foreign to Carroll Ann and myself. As Catholics we attended church with our heads bowed and solemnly attended Mass, and then for the most part went our separate ways. As one of my lifelong friends has said, "When I go to Church I just want to be with God. I don't like all of that hand shaking and talking. When mass is over I'm ready to go home." I wondered when the Bible class would start.

Carroll Ann and I were attentively listening when Joel, in the middle of his 15 minute lesson, suddenly made a statement that would change our lives forever. He said, "Man is not saved by his good works, but he is saved by accepting Jesus Christ as his Lord and Savior." Carroll Ann and I instantly looked at each other in disbelief. Not saved by his good works? How can that be? What about all the good people we knew had lived? Many of them were not Christians. Were they lost? Surely he did not mean what he had said. I knew that later in our stay this would be a major topic of conversation.

When we arrived at the lake Sunday afternoon we sat in the parlor and talked about God. The spiritual discussion was non-stop for the next three days. God was all we talked about. The conversation turned to Jesus Christ and being saved. After a lengthy debate, Joel said, "Nathan, I agree with you. If I had written the rules I would have written them like you are thinking. But I didn't write the rules. God revealed his

Word in the scriptures, and they say that the only way to salvation is through Jesus Christ. It's the only game in town."

I was without a retort. I knew that I had barely read anything of the New Testament. I certainly was not is a position to debate a Bible class teacher of 15 years. However, I now knew where I would go to find out who Jesus Christ was - The New Testament. It never ceases to amaze me to what lengths God will go to make a point and to teach a lesson. I suspected that as later events unfolded, as usual, God would allow me to reciprocate some much needed support to Joel. That would come in later reunions.

This may be the appropriate time to elaborate on that aspect of our relationship. Joel's successful business had two divisions, sportswear and sports equipment. The sportswear division was slowly killing him. His blood pressure was up, he didn't sleep well and he knew he had to do something, but he could not bring himself to let it go. I suggested to him that God might have more important things for him to do, but that until he let this problem go he would not be able to follow God's lead. He slowly began to pray about it and ask for help and guidance. A few months later Joel called to tell me that one morning at 3:00 a.m. he had awakened with a start. Two hours later he received a telephone call from one of his managers that his sportswear warehouse, the one causing his stress and anxiety, had been struck by a tornado and was a total loss. I responded with an instant "praise God." Joel said I was the only person he had related this story to that thought this was a blessing. Later his insurance settlement allowed him to walk away debt free and he has gone on to run the remaining sports equipment division that he enjoys. Truly the Living God is an awesome God to those who put their trust in Him, and see His living presence in their daily lives.

As we were leaving in their van for our return trip home, Joel and I were in the front talking and Carroll Ann was in the back with Lee. As we drove Lee asked us if we wanted to go with them to the Holy Land that November. I had never liked traveling. I particularly did not like traveling into terrorist countries. We stopped for a snack and Carroll Ann took me aside and told me that, in her private conversation with Mary Park earlier that year, Mary had told her that she saw Carroll Ann in the Holy Land in late 1994. I immediately agreed that we should go. It would be a fantastic, although very tiring, experience. We would both re-accept Jesus on the trip and I would find out, once and for all, I was recovered and I had a very strong and healthy heart. But I'm jumping ahead of my story.

God's planning never ceases to amaze me. We left the Jennings' place and headed home for four or five days, then we were off to Maine for a four-week vacation in a rented cottage on Penobscot Bay. I picked up the mostly unread Bible Carroll Ann's mother had given me several years earlier and headed for four weeks of intense scripture study. I had traveled to Minnesota to visit friends we had not seen in 25 years to learn the source of who this Jesus Christ really was.

We stayed in a rented cottage in Bayside, Maine, that had been newly renovated and was very nice. It had a great new den with glass all across the back and a great new master bedroom suite. I spent about four to five hours a day for four weeks not just reading the entire New Testament, but really studying it. My previous studies and experiences of the metaphysical brought the Gospels to life. The Miracles of Jesus' cures and exorcisms were totally real to me. The Bible, I have commented, is the most metaphysical book ever written. I took copious notes. I spent my energies trying to study the similarities between the Christian scriptures and what I had learned in my intense study and experiences in the metaphysical. Cutting through semantics and denominational idiosyncrasies, there are only two real discrepancies I can find. The first is the issue of Jesus being the Savior versus being a great prophet (no small discrepancy), and the second is reincarnation. Some believe Jesus addresses this himself when he appears in different bodily forms to his disciples. Jesus also refers to John the Baptist being the reincarnated Elias (Matthew 17:9-13). According to Saint Paul, in Romans 14, accepting Jesus is the only thing we, as Christians, need to be concerned about. Everything else we believe or do is trivial.

I have come to understand the spiritual world exists for both Christians and non-Christians. There is a distinct differentiation between being "tuned into the spiritual world" and "being saved." They are two distinctly different issues. You can be tuned into the spiritual world and perhaps not be saved, and you can be saved, but not tuned into the spiritual world. Or can you?

The Feather

I remember the day I finished the New Testament. It was in the middle of our last week in Maine. Carroll Ann was sitting at the dining room table working on some family business. I closed the Bible and sat there for a few minutes trying to absorb all that I had learned these past weeks. I got up and walked past Carroll Ann to the sliding glass door. It was a typically cool, breezy August day in Maine. I had a hand on each side of the sliding door opening and I leaned out to breathe in the fresh salt air. I looked around at the large pine trees just 40 feet in front of me. It was good to be alive and to finally know about Jesus. It was good to know the reality of the spiritual world.

I looked around and something caught my eye in the tops of the 75 foot pines that stood in front of me. I saw no bird or animal, but a rustling of a limb. Then in the glint of the sun I saw something floating near the top of the pines. I recognized that it was a small feather. It was caught up in the substantial wind that always blows off the bay. The little feather was twisted this way and that. It moved to one side and then the other. A slight breeze would lift it, and then another would spin it downward. I was transfixed on the little feather as it made its way down. As it got about half way down, I knew what was going to happen. Still the feather was buffeted this way and that. Ever closer to the ground it came. Ever closer to the doorway where I stood. No matter how many times the little feather changed directions it continued towards me in the open doorway. Finally without moving my position I put my "good hands" together and the feather nestled softly in my palms. I looked up to the tops of the pines. I was aware that something mystical had happened, but even to this day I have not heard anyone explain what the feather means.

At the time of this happening I had not seen the movie Forrest Gump. In the movie, Forrest is portrayed as a bumbler who always comes out smelling like a rose, in spite of himself. I prefer to think of him as a classic example of being encircled by the grace of God.

In the movie, the wind blows the feather to Forrest as he sits on the bench relating his outrageous stories to whoever will listen. He is on his way to see his Jenny, little knowing what lies ahead of him. Forrest has always done what he wanted to do. His heroics always come instinctively. Now he is being asked to take on responsibility for Jenny and his son. He takes on that responsibility and, as he places young Forrest on the school bus for the first time, he sheds tears of joy in the knowledge that he has successfully seen Jenny to her final resting and he knows his small son will be socially acceptable. As he watches young Forrest get on the bus, the feather slips from its place in his book and once again is airborne in the wind, ostensibly to find another lost soul to guide. The feather seems to symbolize a presence that will help in setting a soul on its path and staying with that soul until the mission has been completed, or perhaps more correctly, until the soul finds its intended path.

To this day I'm not sure what the feather means for me, but I knew then, and I still know now, it was both a beginning and an end of missions. Perhaps the completion of studying the scriptures and where that knowledge would take me is the best scenario I can envision. The feather resided in our bedroom bookcase within a picture frame on a matted background until one Saturday afternoon in December 1999. As I reflected on the incident in Maine I wondered if the feather should be locked up where it could not do its thing. I was confronted with the thought "like a bird in a gilded cage." That afternoon Carroll Ann and I went riding in the country to look at land. As I got out of the car to take a picture, I removed the feather from my shirt pocket and gently released it to the wind from whence it came.

Our stay in Maine over, we returned to Memphis, rich in the newly acquired knowledge of Jesus and the Word of God. I still had my office at our home.

My son was running one company, and my long-time employee and friend, Mike, was running our consulting/engineering company. A day or two after we returned from Maine a young man called on the telephone. He was from the Department of Commerce in Washington, D.C. He was interested in talking with me about industrial wastewater treatment. He was specifically interested in convincing me to apply my environmental design experience in Mexico. His name was Donald. Thus began a spiritual experience of my meeting a saintly Irish priest named padre Quinn and a beautiful Mexican family that took my wife and me into their hearts and home. It would eventually include Mike being transplanted from the States to find a new life, wife and two baby girls over the following five years, but that is another story.

CHAPTER 11
FELLOWSHIP THAT
CARRIED ME

In the fall of 1994 Carroll Ann and I had returned from the wonderfully revealing trip I describe later, to the Holy Land. Under the guidance of Joel and Lee Jennings we had both reaccepted Jesus as our Lord and Savior on the trip. If you have followed the chronology of the happenings in the past 18 months of my life perhaps you can empathize with my bewilderment at the sequence of the sometimes bizarre spiritual experiences, beginning in May of 1993.

I was now officially retired and I spent my days contemplating God. What was the meaning of my experiences, and what did God have in mind for the rest of my life? These were perhaps the best days in my recent memory. I was physically well and feeling strong again since climbing Masada. I was relaxed and stress free and I felt close to God.

One day, in passing, my wife mentioned that she had spoken with one of our neighbors, a volunteer worker at an inner-city Methodist Church. She had told Carroll Ann about two small inner-city churches, one African-American and one white, which were attempting to merge. She went on to say how poor this little church was, and how the young pastor had really influenced her life in the understanding of helping and giving to others. It was a few evenings later, at our neighborhood Christmas party in early December 1994, that I too met Beth. We talked at length about this inner-city church. As related earlier, my interest since 1983 was the alleviation of hunger of the less fortunate.

The next morning I called and made an appointment to visit the church and meet the young pastor, Reverend Billy Vaughan. Billy was a pleasant, retiring young man in his 40s. His beard and demeanor led me to believe he may have emerged from the '60s. Over the years I was to learn that under the right circumstances Billy was anything but retiring and he did come out of the early '70s generation.

I told him my wife and I would like to donate hams or turkeys for his Christmas baskets. We talked a while and he showed me his food pantry that was scantily stocked with a few of the most basic items. I asked him what his monthly food budget was and he replied $50. I told him we would like to send him money for his pantry on a monthly basis and that we hoped he would use it to feed the poor in his neighborhood. He enthusiastically accepted our offer and introduced me to a young man who was responsible for their food ministry. I was to learn many lessons from this simple first meeting, and from meeting the young food minister, Norman Redwing.

There are many sources of food available to church and other faith-based institutions if they are truly interested in feeding the poor. In Memphis an organization called The Food Bank has a handling fee of $0.11 per pound to qualified institutions. That means you can acquire 100 pounds of food to feed the poor for $11.

I would soon find that what God really had in mind for us was empathy for inner city children. Though we had no inclination at the onset, we soon found ourselves in the middle of several inner city Protestant youth ministries. Norman was the first of several young African American adults I would meet who would dedicate their lives to help the inner city youngsters find God and meaning in their lives. Norman is a recovering street person. To this day he is the only person I have met who could squeeze more blood out of a turnip than I can, and we often joke about that. Norman's passion for helping children at high-risk is exceeded only by his faith and commitment to God. He and I would share many sessions of mutual encouragement as the years unfolded. God would choose me to be one of the persons who would help Norman see that his trials as a youngster, and later a street person, made him immanently qualified to deal with young drug and alcohol abusers. As a child he had spent his after school time under the Mississippi River Bridge just to have a safe place to be. This experience as a youth now drives him to provide a safe place for latch key children and children from drug and alcohol abusive homes. God's economy always amazes me.

He never wastes our learning experiences. As I have grown older I have more readily been able to see this in my experiences with others. As a young person, struggling with life at a basic level, I lost sight of this kind of understanding.

If I have been of any help to Norman, he has helped me even more. His infectious dedication to helping children is contagious and as time passed I found myself much more personally involved with these inner city youth ministries. This has not always been on the physical level, but certainly my conscious awareness and concern for him and his "children" has grown with each passing year. It all started with Billy Vaughan introducing me to this part Native American Indian, part African-American young man who loves God and His children.

So began a lifetime commitment for us, driven by the thought, "An empty stomach can hear nothing good, much less the Word of God." The Billy Vaughans and Norman Redwings would pull us into the ministry of inner city youth. It would change the way I would see life and its meaning over the next seven years. It would lead to our involvement in other similar ministries and finally a lifetime commitment my wife and I made in participating in the reopening of nine inner-city Catholic elementary schools. Some had been closed for 20 years

Shortly after meeting Billy Vaughan in the fall of 1994, it occurred to me that I would like to try my past 18 months experiences on someone I then termed "a traditional minister." Little did I know that "traditional" was not the appropriate label for Billy. Nevertheless, God in His wisdom led me to him. I invited him to our home and began to cautiously unfold encapsulated versions of the stories that you have read about in the previous chapters. I remember talking with him when I began getting the mental block I often get when someone disagrees, or does not believe what I am saying. I stopped and asked him if he was having trouble accepting my story. He said no, far from it, but he had been consciously distracted to think that I should meet a friend of his, a man named Al Holliday.

Within a week Al came to visit me at our home. Al's background was the antithesis of Billy's. He was about seven years older than me, a pleasant man, who had seen the world and would soon change mine. I don't remember his exact words. They don't matter. What impressed me and changed my life was the manner in which he walked into a stranger's home, sat on my couch and proceeded to tell me of his former life of drinking, carousing, and sin in general. I had never encountered anyone who was so willing to be so vulnerable in front of a stranger. In that moment my life changed. I knew that to communicate with others at a meaningful level, one had to be willing to share one's innermost secrets with the other people. If you want to know another person, really know another person, you must first be willing to share yourself, with no holds barred. It is a terrifying thought to most of us who have come to believe that to be vulnerable is to show weakness, and to invite rejection. Yet quite the opposite happens when I truly am seeking the truth and am truly interested in sharing meaningful experiences with others.

As he was leaving my home Al, asked me if I would like to participate in a newly formed men's "small group" being formed at his church. I eagerly accepted and attended the first meeting that very evening.

There were eight men at the first meeting. Surprisingly, I felt welcomed and comfortable even though I was not a member of their church or denomination, and Al was the only one I had met. I would later come to realize the friendliness and fellowship Al showed me was very reflective of his church and every other Methodist congregation I would encounter. Their pastor would also be the facilitator for the group over the next two years, until he departed for a new assignment in another city. Mike never imposed his pastoral position. Quite the contrary, he wanted to be part of the group, something I could accept, but later I found the men in his church had trouble allowing him to step down from his assigned pastoral pedestal.

I have reflected on that group of men that met every other week for over two years. We had the right formula. I had never participated in such a group, but

I can testify to its effectiveness in my life. We started by going around the circle of men and briefly telling something about our personal life. That is difficult for some, but it sets the tone for sharing. One of the cardinal rules for such a group is that no details shared within the gathering leave that room. It is called confidentiality and mutual trust. Without it, a group will quickly wither and die.

As the weeks unfolded, each member would be assigned, or volunteer, to be the leader for the next meeting. We referred to it as "where the rubber meets the road." We would pick a scriptural verse that had special meaning for us, or we were struggling with, and spend about 30 minutes telling the group about our problem or concerns. The group would then ask questions and comment on their feelings and intuition. Most of the men started slowly and cautiously, but as time went on and the trust factor grew, we felt free to delve deeply into the personal natures of each of our problems and struggles. For me it was extremely effective. Joe spoke of the Bible being a manual or a set of "architectural plans" for life. John likened the revelations in the Bible to "hitting a home run." Mike related how dealing with the little things in life is hard as we wait for God's direction. Al spoke of moving through life as "sailing in irons." Mark related "we should fix the roof of our house before we are concerned with the harvest." Don spoke of "childhood molestation," and Bob talked about being given "a second chance" with his illness. All of these stories resonated with me and taught me to consider and understand that everyone seeking God bears his own specifically designed cross.

Being of Catholic upbringing, I was totally unfamiliar with the sharing of sins with other lay persons. Catholics only confess to priests. I came to learn that verbal confession to any other human is the beginning of healing. It is essential to healing. The Catholic sacrament of Reconciliation is an extraordinary source of grace and healing, but my experiences lead me to understand that any verbal confession from one human to another is acceptable to God. It is revealed in the Bible when Jesus tells His disciples "whatever sins you shall retain, they are retained, and whatever sins you shall forgive, they are forgiven." If we are to be Christ-like then we must be willing to forgive, not only those who have sinned against us, but to be willing to listen and help those who confide in us to forgive themselves. We cannot accept forgiveness of others until we can forgive ourselves. This is the beginning of the healing process.

For the next few years my wife and I would be embraced and nurtured by this community of friendly and outgoing Christians. We found great comfort and spiritual growth attending the weekly potluck dinners every Wednesday evening, followed by a spirited Bible class. It was here we learned to reach out and communicate with other Christians, to share the dreams and problems we observed in the world.

I found my lack of scriptural depth led me to study the New Testament with more fervor. I had only begun studying the New Testament in the summer of 1994. I had much to learn and many willing teachers as I strove to know more about God and His Word for me. I began reading the Bible daily, a habit that has stayed with me all of these years.

These were exciting spiritual days for me. I absorbed the witnessing of these good people as they shared their love and compassion in Christ for us. It was this time in my life that I was nurtured by their fellowship. The bridge between my metaphysical experiences and Christian faith was being built, one lesson at a time.

Carroll Ann and I strongly considered joining the Methodist church that was so good to us. We finally understood that St. Paul's words in Romans 8 are just as meaningful today as they were when he wrote them for his early gentile Christians. We may have many differences in how we give honor and glory to God but there is only one significant truth that we must always hold above all else. As Christians we have accepted Jesus Christ as our Lord and Savior. We sit with Jesus now, at the right hand of the Father, part of the Body of Christ. Everything else, including our differences, is trivial and meaningless.

We would remain Roman Catholics but we would hold the love of these people in our hearts as a blessing that can never be taken from us. We learned many things about reaching out to the less fortunate. The Methodists we met truly lived up to their name. They were active in the inner city where it is difficult for the poor to think beyond their next meal, much less worrying about what God has in mind for their lives. The Evangelicals live up to their names in spreading the Word of God and salvation through His Son. Several years later, when the Catholic Diocese of Memphis reopened nine inner city parochial elementary schools, we knew that God had prepared us for a lifetime commitment of supporting those children who could not afford to pay for their school lunches.

It has been a long story that is just beginning to be told. In the winter of 2001 the superintendent of Catholic Schools asked me to write down my thoughts on the re-opening of the inner city schools. Below are the thoughts I wrote.

"In the *fall of 1999 when Carroll Ann and I read about the re-opening of the nine Jubilee schools we immediately felt called to participate in this rebirthing. Our involvement with inner city children had begun seven years earlier. With no agenda or plan we found ourselves involved with several inner city non-Catholic churches that were making efforts to counsel and work with young teenagers in underprivileged parts of Memphis. Soon we realized that at each of these churches we found ourselves working with one of the young adults sponsored by the Urban Youth Initiative. These young adults are in training to determine if their life's work will be with underprivileged children. The words that drive us are "an empty stomach can hear no good, much less the Word of God." So providing food to these fledgling programs became our way of helping. Three things children love are food, music and athletics."*

"I called Dr. Mary McDonald, Superintendent of Schools for the Catholic Diocese, and met with her. One meeting and a look at the mission statement hanging on her wall let me know the lady has a vision for where the schools are going. My wife and I had agreed that our support for this Herculean effort would be to provide a good meal to the children who "would fall between the cracks." One third of the children can afford the meal, another third qualify for government subsidy and the other third must depend on private sector help. We made a lifetime commitment to this end by establishing a charitable remainder trust that will fund what Dr. McDonald's staff has coined "The Angel Food Program." We sought and found guidance on how to structure, fund and monitor the trust through The Hope Christian Community Foundation. The Foundation also administers the trust for us."

"The schools have made a great start, but like anything that is dynamic, new needs and opportunities become evident and require someone, or some group, to step up and fill that need. It takes little imagination to realize that as these nine schools open, grade by grade the numbers and dollars become significant.

There will be the opportunity for someone to provide advanced teaching technology hardware and training, computers and computer training; athletic equipment and coaching; books and librarians. The list is as endless as each of the special gifts of the Memphis citizenry. Some give money, some give time and some give talents. It comes together to form a cohesive, effective body."

"When we saw the gift of the Jubilee blanket we were both amazed that someone had been bright enough to conceive the idea. We were even more amazed that it had become a reality. Our first reaction was to look for "our schools". I had attended Little Flower for six years and then Blessed Sacrament. My wife had attended eight years at Little Flower. The blanket took us back to our beginnings. It brought to our consciousness the realization that the schools that served us so well and were so influential in whatever success we have achieved as citizens of Memphis were being presented with an opportunity to do it all over again. The blanket represents the fabric that has been woven within our lives and it represents the future fabrics that will result from this endeavor. I wanted to hang it at our business office, Carroll Ann took it to a Madonna Circle board meeting where the emotion was magnified by the number of women who had also attended the schools."

"Ten months ago Carroll Ann, by chance, or by divine guidance, attended a Madonna Circle (a Catholic

women's organization) monthly meeting. To her total surprise and astonishment she came home as co-chairman of the yearly Antique Show, the largest of its kind in the Mid-South. Having chaired the show 20 years ago we looked at each other and knew it would be a year that would challenge our patience, endurance and commitment. The primary recipient this year just happens to be the Jubilee school endowment fund. To say we are engrossed is an under statement. The yearly Antique Show will be held the weekend of February 24. Perhaps then our lives will return to some level of normalcy."

"We believe that the Jubilee schools are bigger than being Catholic. God is calling all of Memphis to come together in perhaps the most significant ecumenical and civic challenge of this city's history. Indeed, perhaps a model for city's around the country. We Catholics, historically a reclusive, religious minority denomination in Memphis, need to realize the city is reaching out to us for what we do best, teach young people to believe in God, themselves and their future. We Catholics need to understand we cannot do this by ourselves. There is significant financial support in the non-Catholic sector of Memphis for the reopening of the Catholic Schools. The community at large appreciates the impact that Catholic education has had on our community in the past. They know the public schools do not work for everyone. The important thing is that we ARE, and all we ARE is what God calls us and allows us to be. Together with others from all

backgrounds, races and creeds, that see the vision of truly breaking the cycle of poverty and despair, we are joining together to make it a reality. Each person, each group has a passion and gift that can help make the vision a reality."

"The vision of the Jubilee Schools is a happening that will enhance how the world looks at Memphis. Will this program replace the public schools? I think not. I believe it will provide a blueprint for success that concerned citizens of Memphis and the public schools will observe and come to their own decisions about its effectiveness. A lot is happening, a lot more is yet to be done. We hope our story will encourage others to come forward and give back some of what they have been blessed with."

"I think the most poignant comment I have heard concerning the problems facing the schooling of our country's children was made by a caller to the Larry King show shortly after the Columbine tragedy. With all the high profile guests talking about metal detectors, guards and the like she simply commented, "We took God out of our schools 25 years ago, and until we put Him back, we can expect no better."

Nathan

Nathan Pera, Sr.

PART II

Nathan Pera, Sr.

CHAPTER 12
THE BRIDGES – COMING HOME

Story # 1
The Holy Land

In November 1994 my wife and I flew to Minnesota for a two-week trip to The Holy Land. Joel and Lee had helped us book the trip with a group that had a terrific tour guide. We stayed with our friends in their home that Saturday night and boarded a plane the next evening for Amsterdam and then on to the Holy Land. It was a long trip that I would do differently if I do it again. The trip was about 32 hours from start to finish and, as usual, Lee was the only one of the four of us who slept. We had an eight-hour lay over in Amsterdam and instead of renting a room to catch some much needed sleep we all agreed to go on a rather uneventful tour of Amsterdam.

We landed in Tel Aviv late that night, some 32 hours after our initial departure, stumbled into a nice hotel and had no trouble falling asleep. We were up early the next morning and by 8:00 we were on our chartered bus and heading north along the Mediterranean Sea to our first stop in Caesarea. For the next five days we headed inland to the east until we reached the northeast corner of Israel at the Jordan River. Then we headed south along the West Bank, and finally to the Dead Sea, where the more adventurous displayed their inability to sink in its salt rich waters.

It was not only inspiring but very educational. There was only a sprinkling of inhabitable oases. Seeing the land and the mostly barren terrain it became more understandable why land is at a premium and is constantly fought over in this part of the world. The feeling of history was undeniable.

One of the true gifts on this trip was the opportunity to watch and listen to our two dear friends display their Christian leadership, each in their own way. Joel led the group in prayer at each historic stop, and Lee led us in Christian hymns during the long dusty bus travels along the Israeli countryside. It was truly moving and inspirational. I knew in those few days that I yearned for that kind of relationship with God. I can't say that I have grown in the ways I envisioned, but as I have come to realize these eight years later, God's idea of growth and leadership, and even relationship, is most often different from what I had envisioned. The single greatest stumbling block I have encountered in pursuing God is to think God will communicate with me in the way He communicates with others. God communicates with each of us in His own manner and in the manner that we are most likely to know He is calling us. St. Paul, in Corinthians and Romans 12 of the Bible, addresses the holiness of all the spiritual gifts and how we as recipients are not all called to have the same attributes and gifts. Like the parts of our human body, together we all make up the Body of Christ, sitting now, with Jesus at the right hand of the Father. God is not the God of the dead. I cannot wait until my deathbed is staring me in the face before I strive to meet and know Him and His Will for me. Today is the day. Today is the beginning. Today is the first day of the rest of my life. God calls me, through His son Jesus and His Holy Spirit's guidance, to seek and accept the many blessings He wants to give me. It is so well spoken in the little prayer of Jabez, found in the easily readable book by Bruce Wilkinson, The Prayer of Jabez. Here is the prayer as found in 1 Chronicles (4:9).

"Oh God, that you would bless me indeed!
Increase my territory.
That Your Hand would always be with me.
Keep me from evil,
That I would cause no pain.

I pray this prayer every morning. God has continually enlarged my territory. His hand is always with me, as it has always been. I ask Him to protect me from evil so that I will cause no pain to myself, or others.

One of the stops before Jerusalem was the Mountain of Masada. This was where my gift from God would be manifested on this trip. It would be another life changing experience.

We were waiting in line for the tram to the top of the mountain that is about 3000 feet in elevation. Three of Joel's young friends (early 30s) passed by us and casually asked him to climb the mountain with them. He said sure, and turned to me and said "come on Nathan let's do it." I looked at Carroll Ann. Neither of us thought about my four years of illnesses, and how over-extended physical activity led me to succumb easily to fatigue. It was understandable for me, because I am known to be a little slow, but for Carroll Ann's mind to be veiled took an act of Divine intervention. Finally, Lee made the deciding comment when she said, "Go ahead Nathan, it'll be fun." I often remind her of her many spiritual gifts; prophecy is not one of them.

So up the mountain I headed, dumb and happy. It wasn't long before I realized what I had gotten into. Three of the group, including Joel, went briskly ahead. One of the young women was having a difficult time. It gave me the reason to stay behind, and the reason to go ahead. She needed my help. (Right!!!!). We would walk a bit and then rest. I learned to literally put one foot in front of the other. I dared not look up. In all my youth and athletics I have never hit the wall like I did on that mountainside. I was half way up and wondering what was I doing there at 55 years of age. I began thinking about my perceived heart problems.

About the easy fatigue that I had encountered for the past four years and how any prolonged activity overtaxed my stamina. I was too far up to turn and go back down the mountain. Besides God had sent me this helpless young woman who needed my help. We would climb a bit and then I would say, "You look like you could use a little rest" and we would rest a minute and then continue on. Her need for me sustained me through one of the most demanding physical activities I had ever engaged in.

I never had the first chest pain. I was totally exhausted but we pressed forward. She was just as happy to have me with her as I was to have her there. Finally we made the top. We were obviously the last two of the group to reach the top of the mountain. I sat for a few minutes, my body shaking from fatigue and in disbelief from either why I had been so foolish or how we had actually made it to the top, wondering what would be the repercussions of this overexertion. I had a sandwich and a bottled drink. The group stayed on top of the mountain sightseeing for about an hour. By the time we were headed down, on the tram this time, I was completely recovered. I never had a moment's regret or fatigue. I still have a picture of the "Five Mountain Climbers."

I believe that climb was to prove to me that I did not have a heart problem and that I was strong enough to move forward with my life. Israel was a long way to go to learn that lesson, but it was well worth every mile. I was back.

The last part of our trip was so special that it is hard to recount in words. We had been on the road for five days, staying in a different hotel each night. We were excited but tired too. I will never forget the feelings everyone had, as we knew we were approaching Jerusalem. It was like wow!! All of the sights and memorable occurrences and yet we were just arriving at the Holy City itself. I had the feeling that I would spiritually burst if anymore blessings fell upon me.

We arrived in late afternoon and checked in. Everyone took a brief rest and then gathered for a short excursion around the hotel. We ventured a block or so and found an outdoor ice cream parlor. The six of us sat around a table and began relaxing and enjoying our observations of the locals. It was one of the most impressive experiences I have ever had and it still resides in my mind. All of the young Israelis, both men and women, carried automatic rifles, and as they enjoyed their desserts they simply laid the rifles across the tables in front of them. They are never without their weapons. I have never forgotten that feeling that came from that survival awareness. The Jewish people are truly in a constant fight for survival and have been since their flight from Pharaoh with Moses.

The days in Jerusalem were exhilarating and educational. If you've not been there and are at all interested in the history of the three major religions of the world, go if you get the chance.

The first night we drove to the "Wailing Wall" because we knew that would be where our tour of the city would begin the next day. It is impacting for an American because most all of the TV footage we see shows the "Wailing Wall" as a backdrop for the commentator. It is one thing to see it on TV; it is quite another things to stand and pray next to a local Jewish man and realize you are standing in the midst of your religious heritage.

We had an excellent tour guide, whom we later learned was not Christian, but certainly knew his way around the city. He knew when certain sites would be crowded and he maneuvered us around so that we never waited long at any of our destinations.

Almost all of the buildings of Jerusalem are constructed of a light native stone. The color of the city is awesome. It is hard to realize that three of the major religions, the Jews, Muslims and Christians, claim it as their heritage. As we wandered through the market places in the Old City we discovered the dress has not changed. The feeling of 2000 years ago is still there.

Carroll Ann and I both reaccepted Jesus as our Lord and Savior on the trip home. Our salvation was renewed and Mary Park had a direct influence on our being there.

So many non-Christians played a part in that year. Jim Meade is a Christian, but non-practicing. Richard and Betty are Jewish, and Danny a non-Christian. Of course our Christian friends, the Jenningses had even bigger parts at the finale of this period as they introduced us to the scriptures, and led us to the Holy land and back to Jesus and His Sacred Heart.

This experience led me to believe and often ask: "who is God using in my life today?" I try to keep my eyes open to everyone who passes my way, knowing they have something God wants them to say to me. I never know when that time will come. Perhaps like the Jenningses, whom we met and knew for a brief 15 months in the early 60s, and then didn't see for 25 years, (Ecclesiastes 3:2) ". . there is a time to plant and a time to harvest . . ."

I have learned life is a two way street. We have something to learn and/or teach everyone we encounter in our journey back to God's eternal embrace. The mustard seed I plant today will be the shade tree someone rests under tomorrow. In God's economy it is always a win-win if I just let it be. Be it personal or business, God expects me to see His Son in everything I do and everyone I meet. It's a lesson we all have to learn, whether we believe it needs to be in this life, or like some of my metaphysical friends, if we believe we will be back again.

While researching this story I found the following letter I had sent to our friends shortly after our return from the Holy Land.

Dear Joel & Lee;

Arrived home safely yesterday afternoon. We went to sleep about 7:00 pm and I was awake from 2:30 am on. Jet lag.

We cannot tell you how much we enjoyed being with you for the past two weeks, especially sharing your home with us in the middle of getting your selves ready for the trip.

When I woke up this morning and was just tossing around I began thinking about our conversation towards the end of the trip. I had been wondering what prompted me to tell you both such details about my experiences. I believe Joel that you spoke it just before you were leaving for work, when you said "pray for us". My spiritual journey has been so strange and I have been struggling to keep on the right track. It suddenly dawned on me that I was looking to the two of you for your spiritual support (prayers).

You cannot imagine how many hours I have struggled over my experiences. As scary as they have been I seem to have found Jesus in the end and after all, that is what it is all about.

I would just like to leave you with this thought. The spiritual world is real. Therefore there is an equal amount of good and evil. This is the natural and supernatural law of God. To experience something that is not of the natural does not automatically make it evil or satanic. I agree it is dangerous and I did not seek out this path. Nevertheless the things that I experienced all ended up for the spiritual betterment of all involved. Satan does not and cannot by definition cause someone to do something that is for their spiritual improvement. That is the basis by which I believe that it was not Satan who led me through this desert, but God Himself. For what reason I do not yet know. I do know he freed me to find His Son and He freed my daughter to live her life without possession. Praise be to God.

Therefore I ask of you both to pray for me as you have never prayed for anyone. Pray that I maintain the presence of God every moment of every day, for that is how often He is in my thoughts. I pray everyday that I will continue to hear the voice of the Spirit of God that I know dwells in all of us. I do hear Him every day and every day brings me new spiritual experiences. They are always good experiences, but they always seem to be so close to the edge.

I could retreat back to the safety of my traditional training but somehow I don't think I have been taken this far to suddenly run scared. For that reason I ask for your prayers as I cautiously walk this path. I appreciate your listening to my story.

Since our trip together I realize that sharing and listening are part of what being a Christian is all a about. You have exercised your spiritual gifts well.

I learned a lot on the trip. It was the first time we have been on a "Christian" trip and I felt privileged to be able to see how leadership is exercised on such outings. As I watched the two of you I felt my time will come and your example was not wasted.

Joel, the climb up Masada was a major break-thru for me. I have not pushed myself physically since 1990 when I had the chronic fatigue. In the past, every time I would push I would have a set back that lasted several days, even weeks. I was not even sore the next day. It was a major physical and mental hurdle for me. I'm sure I would not have gone if you hadn't, and you, dear Mary Lee gave me the final push just when I needed it. Thanks again.

Love ya'll - Shalom

Nathan

Story # 2
Life In The Spirit

In the summer of 1995 Carroll Ann and I had become very active at St. Paul's Methodist Church in Cordova.

We attended Sunday services, and particularly the Wednesday evening potluck dinners and Bible class. The people we met were very open and friendly to us and we got to know some of them quite well. In September we attended a weekend seminar given at the church called "Life in the Spirit." The week-end program was conducted by a charismatic arm of the Methodist church that shared how their experiences with the Holy Spirit changed their lives. The program was conducted by a team, formed of members literally from all across the country. They arrived in Memphis Friday, and for some, met each other for the first time.

There were about 100 of the congregation present at the Friday evening opening session. After the initial tone setting remarks by the team leader, they split us into small groups, each with a moderator, and we learned about sharing our spiritual experiences. It was an enjoyable experience for me. As in any group, some were more willing to be vulnerable than others.

Saturday was an all day, into late evening, affair. Each team speaker was assigned a topic on the gifts of The Holy Spirit and discussed it. Some of the speakers were new and some had been team players before. The most effective ones spent more time relating their personal witnessing. For some of the speakers it was an emotional experience to stand up in front of total strangers and share some of their most intimate feelings, perhaps for the first time.

The leaders were a married couple, and their son was one of the team members. He told his story about the manifestation of his gift from the Holy Spirit. He had participated in a healing service and he related how, as each person came forward, he was given the nature of their spiritual concerns before they verbalized it. A story of knowing about the pain and stress of people around him was similar to my experiences of comforting some of the people I randomly encountered. Several of the church congregation who attended Friday night did not come back for Saturday. My wife and I conjectured the subject matter was too uncomfortable for most who didn't return.

On Sunday morning we went to a Bible class where another team couple spoke, and I remember being moved by his statement "the Bible is alive today just as it was 2000 years ago. It was for then, for now and for all times." He spoke of the reality of demonic possessions now, just as they were true then. Something I had witnessed myself but had never heard another Christian affirm.

At the main Sunday service the pastor opened up the pulpit to any of the congregation who had attended the seminar. I was moved to stand up first and speak to the congregation. I cannot remember the exact words I used, which is often the case when I have been moved by the Spirit to speak. While I was taking a shower Sunday morning I had been mulling over the concept that people are afraid to move out of their comfort

219

zone and that is why they reject the concept of a living spiritual world. I told them I had been scared as I pursued the Will of God. I related how I had learned through experiences that if I truly believe that God is with me, and if I am truly pursuing the Word of God, and the work of God, I could try things that are out of my comfort zone. I said that if I tell God "this feels right and I think it is what you want, and I only want it if it's what You want" that God will protect me. I encouraged the congregation to actively pursue God's Will for themselves by getting in touch with the Holy Spirit, the God who dwells within them.

When we left church I felt emotionally involved. I told my wife that I would love to be part of a team that went around the country talking about Life in the Spirit. Little did I realize how this brief experience would lead me to a later encounter with God.

I let it be known to some of the seminar participants that I would like to participate in a weekend program as a team member. The following year almost to the exact date I would get my opportunity. I had just returned from a week's work in Mexico. We spent three days visiting some old friends in Nashville, and stopped at our lake house for five days on the return trip. My wife called our home and picked up a strange message for me. The caller simply said "I'm looking for Nathan Pera. Call me in Fort Worth, Texas." He left a number, but no name or message. As soon as she told me the message I knew it was about being a team member.

I called the number and, after several conversations directed by this premonition, was able to identify the caller. When I finally spoke with "coach" he told me he had called my home the prior week and had got the message "this number is no longer in service." He said he had put my name aside and went on to fill the other nine slots, but as he tried to fill the tenth and last slot, which was the opening presentation, he could find no one who was available for that weekend. He told me something made him think of me and he decided to try again.

I told him I would be available. He gave me the topic for my talk that was "How the Holy Spirit has affected my life." The talk was to set the tone for sharing. It involved the sharing of a spiritual experience with the Holy Spirit that was life altering. The weekend was to be held in Memphis.

I was extremely anxious about standing in front of a group of strangers, but I was just as excited to share my experiences with the participants. Friday evening coach spoke to the small but enthusiastic congregation at the Oakhaven United Methodist Church in south Memphis. Following his introductory talk we broke up into small groups to begin the sharing process. When the small group sessions were concluded the team re-gathered. Everyone was excited about the high level of spirituality in the congregation.

The next morning at 8:30 I anxiously shared my story of childhood seduction that later led to pornographic addiction and how after two years I was still free of the addiction and closer to God than I had ever been. The church was full of "Amens" and "Praise Jesus." The sharing tone was set.

It would be much later that I would realize that once again God's orchestration is without flaw. Being the first to talk, I was then free of any anxiety about what I was to say and could focus on all that was around me. At lunch I just happened to sit next to the pastor of the little church, Reverend Bev, and his wife. Without any prodding Bev told me about his upcoming medical diagnostic test and that he was very anxious about it. I had endured the same test, a colonoscopy, which produced a benign but pre-cancerous polyp. I assured him the test would be painless and the definitive nature of the camera verses the x-ray was the way to go. He seemed relieved.

Bev then went on to tell me about the history of his tenure at the church and how the older white members were slowly passing away and for some reason, no matter what they tried, they could not entice the African-American neighbors to enter their hallways. I was more attentive now that my presentation as a team member was over. As he spoke I listened and my eyes began to take in all that was around us and I began to assimilate it in my mind. Across the spacious dining room and into the kitchen my eyes found the figure of a young African-American woman who seemed to be in charge of the kitchen. She seemed to be in charge of everything. My mind made a mental note. What a great place to bring children in off the street for a free hot meal. What an energetic young woman to bring it all together.

As Bev talked, my mind's eye could see the answer to his problem of getting neighbors into the facility. It was all right in front of us. Invite the children in for a free dinner, some games, singing and dancing. Mix in some discipline and a few scriptural readings. Sing some hymns. The children will come. Slowly, over time, parents will begin to wonder, "what is happening at that church that has attracted my child?" Slowly, one by one, parents will show up to see for themselves. The word will get out. In homes where parents aren't interested in their children, the fellowship with Christian adults will be a positive influence to counteract negativity at home. A role model is what these children need.

Bev's voice began to fade into the walls of the dining room. I knew why I had really been brought there that weekend. I knew why I was picked to be the first speaker. God had planted the seed in my mind for the program that would revitalize this little church. I was never more fulfilled than at that moment, knowing that God was using me for His purpose.

The rest of the weekend went wonderfully well. The little church was immersed in the presence of the Holy Spirit. I have learned that, where there is faith and the Spirit is recognized and accepted, miracles do happen everyday, all day. When there is unacceptance of God's presence, not much good happens. (Matthew 13:58).

I was off to Mexico on business again shortly after the weekend at Oakhaven. When I returned I called Reverend Bev at Oakhaven Church and asked him if I could visit with him about his concerns for the church. He agreed to meet with me.

His diagnostic test had gone well and he had a clean bill of health. I asked him what he was trying to accomplish at his church. He spoke of the used clothing store they had opened at the church to attract poor people in the neighborhood. It was not working. I briefly told him about another inner city church where we were preparing a free dinner for close to 200 persons, twice a week. I told him of the thought that had moved me for more than a dozen years. "An empty stomach can hear no good, much less the Word of God." I encouraged him to consider starting a youth program and that my wife and I would sponsor the food purchase. They had a great kitchen and dining room. It was the vision I had been given at lunch a few weeks earlier.

Rev. Bev was hesitant and I was beginning to feel sort of aggravated because I knew this would work for his church. Later I realized that he was just being a good steward. Finally I began to recall the lunch meeting he and I had the Saturday during the Life in the Spirit weekend. I told him that I had seen the young lady in the kitchen and that perhaps she would be the one who could head up the program. Not surprisingly, Bev mentioned that I must be speaking of Diane and she just happened to be there that day. (Should I have been surprised?) He invited Diane to join us in his office, introduced us and began to cautiously relate my idea to her. He asked her if she thought we could feed young children in the neighborhood and be successful at bringing them into the building for a youth program. Diane never hesitated. She knew she could do it, and she knew several other women and men in the church who would help her.

And so the program was born. A most unusual call to share an experience with the Holy Spirit culminated in the forming of a youth ministry that today numbers more than 200 inner city children eating, playing, and praying together. Bev has retired and has been replaced by Reverend Sam, who is just as enthusiastic about the children. Diane? Well one day while I was driving with Diane to pick up some donated fresh fruit and vegetables for the children, Diane told me "If I could just pay my bills I would work with these children on a full time basis." A year later Diane received a three-year grant and gave up a very nice paying supervisory position in a nursing home. She has acquired 30 hours towards her college degree and she is an inspiration to everyone who comes in contact with her. Most of all she is a role model to these children who would otherwise be walking the streets in this poor south Memphis neighborhood.

When I got that call to participate as a team member it was totally out of my comfort zone. I was scared. I knew I would stand up in front of a group of strangers and bare my soul as I shared with them the dark side of my life. I never know when and why God is calling me, but it is always for my growth and betterment. If I follow my heart I will see and learn. He is truly the Living God who wants a relationship with each of us, but we have to respond to His calling. And I have learned over and over again, if I listen, He is always calling.

Story # 3
Why I Am a Christian

In the summer of 1996 Carroll Ann and I decided to expand the small lake home we had purchased in 1994. One of our neighbors at the lake had just finished a fairly extensive renovation of their home. We liked the work and decided to use their contractor. In a rural area it is difficult to find a reliable contractor, so we were pleased to find someone who had worked for a friend. My wife and I met with the contractor a few days later. I had some sketches and we told him what we wanted and he proposed a price for the work that we agreed on. Unfortunately, following my neighbor's lead, we left the agreement at a handshake.

Every road we travel down has a lesson during the journey, though we may not recognize it until we have reached its end. The contractor got started later than we expected, but finally everything was underway. It turned out the contractor's younger brother, who was a carpenter, would work as the crew supervisor for the expansion work on our home.

As usual in a project without formal drawings, there were changes and adjustments. We decided to utilize the room in the attic area that was being formed by a first floor expansion, so we changed the pitch of the new roof and that gave us a nice loft area. We agreed on the price of the changes, which I wrote down, but there were no formal change orders.

As time went on, I got to know the young man quite well, and rarely ever saw the older contractor with whom I had struck the original agreement. I spent a lot of time working out the detail changes with the young man. One day, after successfully working out a detail, I made the comment to him, "I really enjoy working with you. In fact I enjoy working with you better than your older brother." I can tell you, never underestimate the significance of sibling rivalry. Apparently, and unbeknownst to me, there was a tremendous rivalry between the two of them. So the first thing the younger one did was run home and tell his older brother that I preferred working with him. However, it would be sometime before this episode would surface.

The job wound down, they did finish up, and we were satisfied. There was a checklist of things that needed to be completed. Finally one day I met with the older contractor and he was incensed about my comment of my preferring to work with his younger brother. So he brought it up and questioned why I had made that comment. I was taken by surprise at his reaction to a seemingly harmless statement. I tried to soft sell the comment, telling the older man the truth. I had not seen him since the onset of the contract. I had been working with the younger man and the comment was meant to show my appreciation for his younger brother's hard work and cooperation.

He didn't like my answer and I suddenly realized the magnitude of the problem between the two brothers. He then brought up questions about the prices he had quoted me, and what they had done and hadn't done as extras. We were a few thousand dollars apart in our final estimates. We parted that day without coming to a final agreement. I asked him to send me an invoice, but he never did. We had given him a checklist of things he needed to do before we considered the job complete. We called several times, but to no avail. All of the items were minor and were things we could easily complete ourselves or hire a local handyman to come in and finish. We ended up doing most of the work ourselves. By the July 4th holiday we completed the list and paid him an agreed settlement.

As that summer went by my disagreement with the older contractor began to prey on my mind and to fester. I had really worked myself into a lather over this seemingly inconsequential incident. I simply didn't like what had transpired.

Having terminated the contractor, we were left to finish off the flooring in the older section of the home, which had a stained and sealed concrete finish. The old flooring had taken a beating during the renovation and it would require my spending hours fastidiously scraping the old polyurethane finish from the old surface before I applied a new finish.

I began to think about the episode with the contractor as I scraped on the floor for hours at a time. The more I recalled the incident the more negatively I began to think. I began to imagine all sort of heinous things he might do to retaliate. I began to imagine that in a small rural community you never know how people will interact with one another. So the obsession began to escalate. It was bad. This went on for about six weeks and every weekend I spent time scraping the finish my obsessive thinking seemed to grow stronger and worse.

I realized this type of thinking was something I had done routinely in life prior to my spiritual awakening, but I had not done this in several years. At some point I remember recognizing what was happening and I spoke to God about it. Somehow I was not upset about what was happening. It was strange. I couldn't understand it, but somehow I had the feeling this episode was going someplace. So, as I prayed to God, I told Him I felt as though I should not fight this feeling, and that I was going to continue to let this happen. I was going to carefully follow this to where He let it lead me. Of course the obsession continued, but for some reason I just didn't seem upset about it. I was confident it was taking me someplace I needed to go.

The obsession continued on in to late summer, and again we were headed up to Minnesota to visit our friends the Jenningses at their lake house. When we arrived we played golf the first day. I remembered that Joel had played better than me. I am only rarely a good golfer and I have never taken scoring or winning very seriously. I'm just not good enough to take it seriously.

I noticed that I had a very negative attitude towards my friend Joel, and that bothered me. That evening around 10 Joel excused himself and headed off to bed. So Carroll Ann, Lee and I continued talking about our lives since we had last met.

At some point I mentioned to Lee that I was really having some negative feelings. I told her I had been having feelings of obsession, like I have a negative presence that was really bothering me. She sat up immediately in her chair and leaned forward and said, "Nathan would you like for me to pray with you?" I responded, "yes of course I would."

So my good friend Lee proceeded to give Satan holy hell. She just ran him up one side of the pole and down the other. She said, "You have no right to be in this man's spirit. He is a child of God. He sits with Jesus Christ at the right hand of the Father. He is washed in the blood of Jesus. Be gone Satan." Lee really exuded fire and brimstone for about five minutes. When she finished I knew that it was over. The negative was gone. I can tell you from that moment on I never had another negative thought or feeling about that contractor. It was just that simple.

Well, I was duly impressed. So as we left the Jennings' home, I remember thinking what a tremendous gift Lee had. I had always known she had been an effective prayer. Some people just know how to pray and God listens to them. That is a gift and I was so impressed that she could run Satan out of my spirit with just five minutes of prayer. Even when we reached home I continued thinking about what she had done. I remember thinking to myself "I wish I had the gift to do that, the power to expel Satan from myself at will." Since my encounter with the demons from my daughter's spirit, I had been truly frightened about Satan's potential effect on my spiritual life, not from a salvation point of view, but from the quality of life he can destroy.

About two weeks later a package came from Lee, and in the package were two books by Neil Anderson, *Victory Over the Darkness* and *The Bondage Breaker*. I looked at the two books and I knew that it was essential that I read one of them first. I picked *The Bondage Breaker*. I read about 40 pages, closed the book and sat back in my chair and said, "wow!!!" In the book was a note from Lee that said, "Nathan I was studying these books and I thought you should have them." So she had been inspired to send them to me.

Those two books really did change my life. Dr. Neil Anderson talks about the reality of demonic possession causing a lot of psychological problems, defying all types of psychiatric care. What really impressed me was the knowledge that as a Christian having accepted Jesus Christ as my Lord and Savior, I had the same power that Lee had exhibited just two weeks before for my benefit. I just needed to take responsibility and to assert my position with Jesus in the presence of God the Father. It was amazing. I found that when tempted by Satan, or feeling the presence of Satan, I could in fact invoke the same results myself.

I told this story to a group of children one evening. I explained the feeling I have about this power in the name of Jesus by telling them this. "If someone came to me and said, 'Nathan you can be one of two things. You can either be a Christian or you can be President of the United States and the most powerful man in the world, but you cannot be both,' it would not take me a split second to choose that I would prefer to be a Christian, rather than to be the most powerful man in the world."

There is absolutely no doubt in my mind that is the decision that I would make, and in fact have already made. The power to rebuke Satan from my life, knowing it is the power I have inherited by accepting Jesus Christ as my Lord and Savior, is the most powerful thing that I could imagine possessing.

So when people ask me if I fear for my salvation the answer is no because I believe the only threat to my salvation was my inability to deal with Satan's temptations. Once I understood that all Christians, in accepting Jesus, have this power and authority to rebuke the presence of Satan, I then knew I was empowered to use my free will to deal with temptation. The rebuking needs to be verbalized aloud. It is a powerful tool. The words for those who might be interested are:

"As a believer that Jesus Christ is the Son of God and my Lord and Savior I am an adopted child of God.

Therefore I sit now at the right hand of the Father, as part of the Body of Christ.

As part of that Body I understand that I have power and authority over Satan, in Jesus' name.

I am washed with the blood of Jesus the lamb. Therefore I take that authority and responsibility and rebuke your presence Satan. You have no right to be in my spiritual space. I rebuke you and command you in the name of Jesus to leave my heart, mind, body and soul and all of those around me."

So I always try to remember that as a Christian I need to understand my position with God through His Son Jesus Christ. It also explains the significance of the name Jesus Christ, uninvited, coming into my mind in the late fall of 1993 It is the reason why I am a Christian.

For me the lesson was that negative obsessions about people or things is the work of Satan. Yet I believe that God allowed the temptation to proceed so that I could learn the lesson. I took the obsession with me to visit our friends in Minnesota, and it exhibited itself around a simple game of golf that allowed me to bring this up to Lee, and she demonstrated to me the power of prayer. Then she further was moved to send me the books, which led me to read and understand the power that comes with acceptance of Jesus Christ as my Lord and Savior.

Now when these obsessions even flicker in occurrence, I recognize them for what they are. They are originated by demonic influences and as long as I stay in touch with God I can overcome those types of temptations, as well as any other temptations that I might be faced with on a daily basis. But I realize I must make the choice to take authority over Satan. God does not make that choice for me.

Nathan Pera, Sr.

Story # 4
Never Say Never

For some reason God has many times chosen physical manifestations to teach me spiritual lessons. Though I am not sure of His reasons, they have always been effective in getting His point across. One such lesson came unexpectedly in the late fall of 1995.

The story begins in the fall of 1994 when the small group at St. Paul's was formed. One of the men had been experiencing a lengthy period of great mental anguish. In reality he was coming out of a very difficult time. The specifics of his mental anguish are of no consequence, and in the spirit of confidentiality, I will skip to the chase.

In one of our small group meetings he revealed that during his struggle of trying to understand the trauma he had endured, he became angry with God. Two of us in the group, in very sincere terms, spoke with him about his anger with God, and we related that we had never experienced enough pain to bring us that level of despair. Further, we both agreed that we could not envision any circumstance that would evoke such an emotion towards God. It would be approximately one year later, in a rather unsuspecting setting, that God would allow me to learn a much needed lesson in humility and to never say never.

I was still involved in the financial aspects of our businesses. We still were entering our invoices manually, which may sound totally archaic, but the reasons are not relevant to this story. The fact that we were manually handling our invoices, receivables, and deposits, is relevant to the story.

Our fiscal yearend occurs November 30, so as November began to come to an end, historically I would lock myself in my home office for a week and reconcile the billings, deposits, receivables and cash. It is a simple fact that invoices minus deposits equals receivables. When you are doing this manually the trick is to get this equation to reconcile. We were issuing thousands of invoices per year, so you can imagine just compiling all the numbers by hand was cumbersome and time consuming. This year would prove to be even more of a headache. I literally would add the invoices until I obtained a repeatable total dollar value. The same objective would be true for all of the account receivable deposits. Finally, we tracked the receivables, and they too had to be totaled until a dependable number was obtained.

I realize this sounds simple, and in theory it certainly is, however year after year it would take a full week of work for me to be comfortable with the numbers and that all transactions were accounted for. This particular year I could not get the reconciliation at the end of the week, so we moved into the second week. The longer it took the more frustrated I would become. This was always the time of year my wife and employees knew to give me a wide berth and leave me alone. When things went slowly, as was the case in this year's tabulation, the frustration easily slid into exasperation

The evening of the tenth day I found my error in computation. It almost always was a simple double addition or subtraction, something that is so obvious, like the forest, I can't see it for the trees. It was around 8 p.m. when I discovered my error and so, rather than work through the details to confirm my enlightment, I gathered all my papers and notes and prepared to recap the financials the next morning.

The next morning I had breakfast and made my usual phone calls to get the day started. By 8:30 a.m. I began to prepare to settle in to complete the financial report. My wife also was working at the house this day, and as I sat down to begin she entered my office with an administrative question. We spent about 10 minutes reviewing her documents and then she gathered them and left me to finish up the yearend work.

I was in a great mood. I had finally gotten over the hurdle and now it was a matter of just consolidating my work into a finished format for our record keeping. I settled into my chair and turned to where I had left the papers the night before. The papers consisted of about 8 to 10 pages and some small note pages. They were not where I had left them. I begin casually looking around. They were nowhere to be found. I am not a "clean-my-desk" sort of person. An organized desk for me is everything in its own neat pile. So I again went quickly through each pile; still no papers. Now I was beginning to think about what was happening. Next I went through each pile very slowly and carefully, feeling sure that I had simply missed the papers that obviously had to be somewhere on my desk. Still no papers.

I got up and went to the kitchen and got a glass of water, then back to my office. I looked again. No papers. Now 45 minutes had elapsed and I was beginning to feel aggravation setting in, when I suddenly had this feeling that God was playing with me. I sat back in my chair and said aloud "Okay, I know you are up to something. I'm cool. I'm not going to get upset. I know these papers are here somewhere." I returned to looking. Now I was looking in my file cabinets. Maybe, I thought, my memory is not so good and I've put the papers away for safe keeping. Nothing.

I got up from my desk and went upstairs where my wife was working and asked her if she had seen the financial papers I was looking for. She said no. I related to her the incident as it had unfolded. She came down with me and began looking around with me. Nothing.

As the minutes turned into hours I was determined not to give in to exasperation. I was convinced that something was going on, but what was it? It was now after 11:30 a.m. and still no papers. I finally lapsed into doubting that I had actually left the papers on the desk, or even had completed the work. Yet all of the work sheets were gone. It wasn't just a summary sheet that was missing. Of course that really made it worse because not only had I lost the summary sheet, all of the data compilation sheets were gone too.

Around 11:30 my wife came into the room and asked me if I had found the papers. I related no and we had an exchange of words that reflected the frustration both of us were feeling. She now had the feeling that she had unknowingly done something to cause me to lose the papers. I dismissed her concern and I told her I knew the papers were here somewhere and I would find them.

I decided a lunch break was the best thing I could do at this time. After lunch I began again looking for the papers to no avail. This went on until about 3 p.m. and now I was really frustrated and exasperated. I began cursing to myself about how stupid I must be to have lost something that took me so long to develop.

About 3:30, and now seven hours into this fiasco, I headed upstairs to our bedroom. I walked in the door from the hallway and Carroll Ann was on the telephone in our sitting room. As I walked past her and turned into our bedroom I lost it. Our bedroom is about 20 feet across and as I stepped into the room I began to really get angry. As I neared the other side of the room I said to myself, "God how could you do this to me?" And as soon as I said those words, my mind was totally occupied by the name and thoughts of the young man in my small group and the words I had said to him, "I could never get angry at God." It was like a huge mental neon sign. I caught myself and corrected myself with the words "No God didn't do this to you, He allowed it to happen to you." No sooner had those last words crossed my mind than I whirled around and in the moments it took me to walk back to my wife in the sitting room the answer to the missing papers came to me.

As I reached my wife she was hanging up the phone. I stopped in front of her and said, "Where is the box you had this morning with the papers we reviewed?" She answered, "I put them back in the attic." "Show me," was all I said. She got up and I followed her into the attic and removed the top from the box. I knew where my financial papers were. I reached into the box and pulled out a large stack of her papers, knowing that my papers were in the bottom. And there they were.

Over the years I have recalled this story many times. It was so amazing to me. In the instant that I said the words in anger, "God why did you do this to me?" The instantaneous mental recollection of my words many months earlier in our small group and my awareness of the folly of those words, followed by my understanding that "No God didn't do this to you, He allowed it to happen to you," I had voiced the anger at God I had instantly been reminded of the suffering young man in our group, and I had learned the lesson, all in that brief moment. As soon as I acknowledged the lesson the location of the papers came to me. By the time I retraced my steps across the bedroom, I knew the papers were in the bottom of the box my wife had brought into my office early that morning. She had placed the box on my desk and removed her papers. In the discussion she had placed her papers on top of mine, which was in the middle of the desk, right where I had left them the night before. When we finished, she simply scooped up the bundle that included my papers and placed them in the box. My papers were in the bottom of the box, and I suddenly knew it.

I had told this suffering young man that I had never been mad enough at God to blame Him for my misfortune. Yet in seven short hours I had verbalized my anger at Him for causing me to lose my papers, a relatively trivial problem compared to the young man's in our group. God had once again taught me a simple lesson in a hands-on experience. I have never ceased to be amazed at the ease at which He slips up on me when I least expect it and gives me a little tweaking. I can tell you that to this day I never say never when someone relates to me some mistake they have made.

Story # 5
The Gift of Mercy

The Gift of Mercy is akin to the Gift of Healing. Mercy relates to the healing of psychological pain and requires the capacity for empathy with the one in pain. From the moment of my awakening in 1993 I had a strong desire to be drawn towards healing, but no matter how much I wanted it, the gift never materialized. There were several opportunities that I tried to pursue, but to no avail. Each time I would attempt to become involved with someone who was physically ill, an obstacle would always surface and the opportunity to participate in the healing of a physical ailment continually eluded me. Later I would come to understand that my Gift of Mercy would be a gift of emotional healing. First I would need to learn more about the structure of energy transfers that occur between humans. Just as there is an energy transfer between human and spiritual beings, there is a transfer of energy in the physical world between humans.

Earlier I briefly referred to the initial learning of this energy transfer in the book by James Redfield, *The Celestine Prophecy*. Knowing about it is one thing, experiencing it is something else. It would take a family trip to Vail, Colorado, to give me the long awaited answer in my search for the gift of emotional healing, the Gift of Mercy.

My wife is a romantic and in the winter of 1998 she decided that our two grandsons needed a memory. The following spring she and I, and our son's family flew to Vail for a week of skiing and fun in the snow.

Our grandsons were then 12 and 8 years of age and the anticipation of skiing with my son and his two boys was an adventure I was looking forward to experiencing. We flew into Denver and transferred to the Eagle Vail Commuter flight. The final flight pattern into Eagle Vail is a beautiful sight, assuming the weather is nice. We arrived on time, and once we had hooked up with our ground transportation, we stepped inside the baggage terminal to await the arrival of our luggage.

I was feeling good. We were on time and things were going smoothly, the way I like it. As luggage began moving out on the carousel I noticed a medium size bag was riding on its edge. I casually reached out to my side to straighten it. I immediately felt a twinge in my lower back muscles. It was just enough to get my attention but it seemed to be of no consequence. We gathered our luggage and started the 45-minute car trip to our hotel in Vail.

The next morning we were up early and, as we were starting to layer dress for the cold Rocky Mountain weather, I noticed that as I struggled with the squeezing into the thin layers of clothing my lower back began to spasm. In my early years I had a history of lower back pains and I know how debilitating it can be. I was not to be deterred. We had come a long way to have a fun family vacation and I was not to be denied. So with aching lower back and two aspirins, the boys and I were off to the slopes.

We skied for two or three hours and I was constantly aware that my back was going to be a problem. We ate lunch on the mountain and skied until about 2 p.m. and I knew it was time for me to call it a day. I told my son I would head down the hill and rest my back for more skiing the next day. I made it down the hill and back to our hotel without much difficulty. But the worst was yet to come. I sat down to rest for about 30 minutes and, once I stopped moving around, my lower back muscles locked up and the pain became almost unbearable. I was in the condo by myself and I knew I needed to get help and relief. I looked through the telephone directory and found a local chiropractor. Luckily he could see me and was less than half a mile from our place. The half-mile walk seemed like a marathon. Each step was agonizing. Finally I arrived and he worked on me. I felt a little better but there was no miracle cure. As I was leaving he asked me where I was from, and I told him Memphis. He related that there was an oriental lady named Nickey that worked with him in his office and that he thought I should see her. I took one of her cards and headed slowly back to our condo.

Always the optimist, I was hoping for the best, but the next morning was really bad. The lower back muscles had really spasmed and I knew skiing was out of the question. The family went off, and about 10 a.m. I decided to call Nickey Ho and see if she could see me. I really had no idea what her specialty was but for some reason I thought I should try and see her. As my luck would have it, she answered the telephone. I began describing my problem to her and she immediately asked me if I had money problems. I related, "Not that I was aware of." She continued and said, in broken English, "You not able to pay me?" I assured her that I could pay for her services and that I really needed to see her that morning. She agreed. I asked her how much she charged for a visit and her reply was, "I will tell you after I see you, how much I charge." At that moment I would have paid any amount if she could help me.

Again I slowly, and painfully, walked the half-mile distance to their offices. She asked me to sit on an examination table and she began walking around me touching my back, arms and shoulders. As she examined me she asked me if I had injured myself in any way. I answered no. She then asked me "Do you believe in God?" When I answered yes, she asked me to tell her what God meant to me. By the time I gave her a five minute theology dissertation she was standing in front of me and she said "This energy no yours." It took me a few seconds to understand what she was saying. She repeated, "This energy not from you, from someone you have been working with." I suddenly now had to assimilate the idea that I was again having a spiritual experience. She continued by giving me the physical description of the man whose energy I had absorbed, that was causing this lower back pain. "He is large, stocky man who has been doing psychological work with you in past six months." She was describing a psychologist acquaintance to a tee. I had been seeing him the past year in an attempt to find direction for my life.

"This man have money trouble. Money trouble causes lower back pain. You have absorbed his pain. I teach you how to release it." She then began an encapsulated lesson on human energy exchanges. This was a subject that I had been keenly interested in for the past five or six years. I had already begun to understand that in daily human encounters people unconsciously exchange energy patterns. The theory of insufficiency surfaces, mostly because of the fear pattern in one or both of them. Humans, on the whole, believe there is not enough of everything to go around, and their reaction is to hoard what they have. That includes air to breath, money to spend, good feelings, and so on. On the flip side, it includes feeling better by downloading negative energies like insufficient money, relationships gone bad, on down the list of personality deficiencies we know exist, to those we encounter on a daily basis. For those readers who are knowledgeable in the Enneagram theory of the nine major personalities, this will come as no surprise. Earlier I mentioned the *Celestine Prophecy* as a good basic illustration of personality interactions. *The Wisdom of the*

Enneagram by Riso and Hudson is a very in depth study of psychological and spiritual growth using the Enneagram theory. *Designer Clothes by God,* written by Sr. Mary Helen Kelley, is a more easily read approach to the nine dominant personalities.

Nickey continued her lesson on energy exchanges. She told me that I was a healer and that I would absorb other energies in my relationships. I needed to understand what was happening and how to release the energies to prevent pain for myself. Then she told me something I have never forgotten and I try to share it with others who are involved in any type of counseling, and physical or psychological healing work. Negative energy is the source of all pain. When my energy flows smoothly, and that includes the energy I absorb from all of the people I contact each day, my body performs well. But when I either do something against the natural, or moral, laws or I am in contact with someone else who is, my energy can become blocked. Blocked energy is what causes stress, that leads to physical pain, that leads to chronic pain, that leads to disease, which can eventually lead to death. In my current writing-in-progress, *Contemplation and the Presence of God,* I expand on this reality and its consequences for counselors and healers alike.

I became deeply engrossed in what she was telling me. I knew from previous experiences that I could absorb spiritual entities, therefore it was not a stretch for me to envision the absorption of negative energies. I asked her to teach me how to release the energies before they started to cause me pain. She smiled and asked me to follow her outside. We walked out into the crisp spring Rocky Mountain air. The freshly fallen night's snow clung to the pines outside her office. She reached up and took a branch of one of the large pines in each hand, closed her eyes and said, "I feel the pain, I understand the pain, I accept the pain, and I am thankful for the pain." She paused for a moment and then continued. "I feel the lesson, I understand the lesson, I accept the lesson and I am grateful for the lesson. Now I release any negative energy back to the universe for the good of the universe." She opened her eyes and turned to me with a smile and said, "now you release this energy that is not yours, back to the universe." I followed her lead and she helped me through the words. When I was finished she told me to come back tomorrow and she would see if the energy had been released.

Before I left her I asked her how much I owed for her services. She said "You pay me one quarter." I thought I had misunderstood her and asked her to explain. She answered by telling me that she sees two kinds of people, those who have experienced the reality of the spiritual world and those who have not. If they have not she charges $100 per visit, because they feel they need to pay money in order to acquire a benefit. For those who have experienced the synchronicity of the universe, she charged a token quarter. I happily paid her the quarter and agreed to return the next day.

Following her examination of me the next day she said "For some reason you are retaining this energy. Are you seeking attention from someone?" She told me that it was now up to me. The energy could only be released when I was ready to let it go. The rest of the week I spent on a heating pad in pain. My skiing was over for the trip and would be limited to the few hours on the first day. On the way home during the flight I meditated on the plane trying to understand why I had not released the pain. Somewhere over the Midwest I received the words "just the messenger." Then I understood that before the energy would be released, I needed to relate the incident to my friend in Memphis. The one who's energy I had absorbed.

The next day I visited him and, as tactfully as I could, gave him the message of what I had learned in Colorado. He maintained he was not having a money problem. I simply replied, "I am just the messenger" and left. That night I had a dream and in the dream my psychologist friend was arguing with his partner who was very angry. In the dream I saw five embossed checks, not the kind you and I would use, but more like government or institutional checks. I returned to my friend and related the dream to him. He never acknowledged anything but I suspect the embossed checks in my dream were possibly insurance payments for patients and this was causing some financial friction between him and his partner. From that moment on our relationship changed. He withdrew psychologically from me, and though our relationship is pleasant, we have never discussed this subject again, and all of our conversations are guarded.

The lower back pain vanished after the second visit. I was thankful for meeting the little Oriental woman in Colorado. As time went on I found the tree release did not work for me. We all have different belief structures, and to successfully enter and participate in the spiritual world, I had to be comfortable with my beliefs. I changed the words she gave me to follow more closely my personal belief in God. The words I use successfully are as follows;

"I feel the pain, I understand the pain, I accept the pain and I am grateful for the pain.

I feel the lesson, I understand the lesson, I accept the lesson and I am grateful for the lesson.

Now heavenly Father, in the name of your Son, my Lord and Savior Jesus Christ, I give you any negative energy, to give back to the universe, for the good of the universe."

As soon as I had learned this technique I began to have healing encounters with many persons. I recognized that I had the spiritual Gift of Mercy and that God had withheld the encounters until I was spiritually ready to deal with the transferred energy that resulted from that type of ministry. I wrote Nickey a letter of thanks for sharing her wonderful gift with me, and I have tried many times to call her, but I have never had any direct correspondence since that week in 1999. I have had many one-on-one experiences with people in emotional pain, and those experiences left no doubt that I could not have gone where those encounters took me without the awareness that negative energy release is essential to my physical health.

My experience has been that the release will not work for me until I truly understand the lesson. That is, if I am feeling a pain and I just assume it is a negative energy I cannot just say the words and the release happens. As time has elapsed I have developed an intuitive feeling when I am encountering a healing episode and usually, but not always, I can intuit the source of the pain fairly quickly. I would encourage all counselors and healers to contemplate a thought. If I am a healer then I need to be mobile and available to those who need me when they need me. Psychological problems of a relationship nature create mobility infirmities. Bone and arthritic problems are the most common manifestations of these types of energy blockages. If I am involved in a healing session with someone I need to recognize it, and I need to clear that energy when our encounter is completed. Nickey told me that I would be able to recognize that a healing encounter was occurring by focusing on the eyes of the other person. She said, "You will know in their eyes when it is happening." I have found that advice to be true without exception.

I have also learned that the longer the negative energy is with me before I am able to release it, the longer the pain takes to subside. When the negative energy is mine I find the same is true. The longer I have resisted responding to the psychological or moral issue that is the cause of the pain, the longer it takes for the pain to be released. This is particularly true for subconsciously generated pain that may have been engrained for years. It may take several days, or weeks, for the pain to be completely released. The healing is always directly proportional to the heart's commitment to release the source of the pain.

No matter what the religious persuasion, be it Christian, Jew or eastern, we should be able to relate to the concept that when we do something against the laws of nature, or God, we will incur some form of divine retribution. This is a foreign concept to most persons in the western culture. If man received a zap of pain every time we did something wrong there would be much less wrong in the world. God does not work on a time schedule as we know it. His reaction to our shortcomings is not usually in vengeful retribution but, rather, comes most often in the form of lessons to be learned. Scripturally, we know God can make the lesson a strong one.

As a Christian I recognize that energy blockage comes from sins of commission or omission. Something I have done or should not have done, or something I should have done. The Gospels are full of incidents

253

where Jesus cures someone of a physical infirmity and then concludes the healing with the admonition, "Go your way and sin no more, lest something worse befall you."

Story # 7
Padre Quinn – The Urgency

It was a cool, sunny, early fall day in late September of 1994. My wife and I had just returned from four weeks in Bayside, Maine, where we had spent our time soaking up the summer cool breezes and temperatures that come off Penobscot Bay. I was feeling exceptionally good from the rest and relaxation. The phone rang in my home office and when I answered there was a young man on the other end. He introduced himself and said he worked for the federal government in Washington, D. C. He said he would like to ask me some questions about industrial wastewater treatment. I remember the moment like it was yesterday. It was one of those defining moments that would significantly alter the course of my life. I simply felt like I should talk to this young man for as long as he wanted to talk. It was the beginning of a journey that would change my life again, and many of those around me.

The first time we talked for perhaps two hours. He indicated he would like to call back at a later date. I agreed. We talked again two weeks later and then in mid October for another two hours. I had become attached to this young man over the telephone. He had an easy manner and apparent enthusiastic interest in my life's work.

He briefly told me the pertinent part of his life story. He had spent time in the Peace Corps and had seen the third world countries that had no running water, no sanitation facilities, and no electricity He indicated his life's dream was to learn about treating water and then return to South America to begin a lifetime of teaching sustainable water purification and sanitation.

In December he and his older cousin flew into Memphis for a visit to see some of our installations and for us to get to know each other face-to-face. We spent three close and intense days visiting a couple of our treatment installations and talking about what might be our future together. We talked about our dreams for the future, and what impressed me most was that all three of us wanted to do something constructive for the less fortunate in the world. The last night the three of us stood on my front steps and savored the moment as we said goodbye. We all knew it was something special. They left with the promise of putting together a business plan for forming a company to treat industrial wastewater in Mexico.

We talked many times during the early winter of 1995, and into the spring when they returned to present their business plan. I knew that I would be hiring the young man as our international sales representative. He spoke fluent Spanish and I knew he had sold me. The unanswered question was "could a young man without specific experience successfully sell wastewater engineering projects to the Mexican industries?" It was then that fate intervened in the spring of 1995. Working hard to impress me that he could make sales happen, he landed a nice job in South America. Everything seemed to be moving forward. The South Americans flew up to Houston and met with our people and it seemed we were off and running. I was sold. If the young man could land this kind of a project without any training or experience, what could he do when we gave him the proper tools?

In June of 1995 we offered him a position. His cousin had decided to pursue another venture. We sat in my home and worked out the company mission statement: treating water in underdeveloped countries and returning a percent of profits to the proximal population. I remember the meeting well because the three principal players all were asked to state what they wanted to get out of the venture. I wanted to make money to help feed the hungry. The young man wanted to treat water in third world countries in a sustainable manner. My long time employee Mike, who joined us, simply wanted to experience the Mexican culture. Little did we all know at the time how prophetic his words would be for himself.

The young man moved to Monterrey, Mexico, in the fall of 1995. It was a stressful time. There were a lot of surprises and unexpected financial expenditures, but we pressed on. By late 1995 we had landed a very nice preliminary engineering study for a Fortune 500 company. The study was successfully executed in

January of 1996. However nothing else developed. I began to sense that something was wrong. For a long time I thought it might be me. Perhaps I was not being committed enough. Perhaps I should be in Mexico with the young man. However, the opportunity for me to move never materialized.

To make a long story short, in the summer of 1996 we were forced to terminate our young friend for lack of business. But God was not to be denied. It would become more obvious as time went by, but apparently he wanted me and my long time employee in Mexico. On the day our young man was packing to leave, literally on the day, he received a telephone call from one of his industrial contacts saying they wanted us to perform a preliminary study for them. The young man gave them our state-side telephone number and he departed Mexico.

I received the call from a British-owned company located in Saltillo, Mexico. They had our proposal for a study and wanted us to come down and execute the work. This is what we had envisioned from the beginning. We were now officially doing business in Mexico. I would be remiss if I did not spend some time talking about the city of Saltillo. I was introduced to the city in a most extraordinary way.

Since my illness in the early 1990s I had no tolerance for the heat. We had spent time in Monterrey in January and it was nearly 90 degrees. Now we were going to

Saltillo, about 30 miles southwest of Monterrey in July. I prayed God would deliver me from the anticipated heat. Mike and I flew into Monterrey late one evening and drove to Saltillo. It was around midnight when we arrived and we were both exhausted, so we paid little attention to much of anything. The next morning we started to the restaurant for breakfast and to meet our new client. As we stepped out into the early morning air we were both surprised by the cool temperature. We acknowledged it, but nothing more. Our client arrived and we had breakfast. Being concerned with the temperature I asked Bill what the day's high temperature would be. He related about 70 degrees. I asked him Fahrenheit or Centigrade? He laughed and said Fahrenheit. He could tell by our expressions we were confused. How could it be 115 degrees in Monterrey and just 30 miles away be 70 in Saltillo? Bill related that Saltillo is called the "air-conditioned city" of Mexico. "We are at an elevation of about 5000 feet and it is always breezy and cool and has a low humidity," he said.

Well, he had not exaggerated. During the three-day study the high temperatures were 70, 72 and 73 degrees. I called my wife and told her I had died and gone to heaven. I fell in love with that city during those three days. I had hoped my wife and I would spend most of the rest of our lives there.

The rest of 1996 my partner and I executed the engineering, equipment procurement and startup of the first of several successful projects for the British-owned company and we had made great friends. We traveled back and forth many times during the rest of 1996 and through early 1997. Saltillo would not only be my favorite city for its climate, I would soon be led to meet a man who would change both my life and my partner's.

What you have read so far was background. Now that you know I was deeply committed in Mexico, it is time to introduce Padre Quinn.

In late summer of 1996 I was jogging near our lake home and I ran into our next-door neighbor about two miles from our homes. We had not seen each other during the summer so we briefly chatted. He asked that Carroll Ann and I come over later in the morning and the four of us would catch up on recent events. When I got home I mentioned to my wife that I felt perhaps our neighbor had something to tell us. My intuition would not let me down.

Later that morning we went to their home and we were sitting around chatting when for no particular reason we started talking about Mexico. It turned out that our neighbor had a cousin who had lived in southern Mexico for the past 30 years. They talked about how great the weather was and they never needed heat or air conditioning. I mentioned that I had recently just returned from a city in northern Mexico with the same type of climate, the city of Saltillo. It turned out that our neighbors had good friends in Tupelo, Mississippi, who spent a lot of time and money supporting an Irish Catholic priest who ministered in Saltillo and the neighboring countryside. They then asked, "You must know Padre Quinn?" I answered no. I had not had the opportunity to meet him. Our visit soon ended and we headed home with the knowledge there was some connection with Mexico.

About a month later I was talking to a business acquaintance and the subject of Mexico came up. He asked me where we were working and I mentioned Saltillo. His immediate reaction was "You must know Padre Quinn?" No, I responded, this time noting that this was the second time I had heard the priest's name mentioned in casual conversation in a relatively short period of time.

I acquired the priest's telephone number from our lake neighbors and after many misconnections I finally talked to Padre Quinn on the telephone. He was a pleasant man and he said he would love to meet us when we were next in Saltillo. We had a trip scheduled in mid October and we set up a Thursday meeting. We would meet him at his parish church and he would take us around the city's barrios (slums). Later, as the trip drew near some of our business meetings were postponed and we were going to be finished Wednesday afternoon. We decided to leave Mexico Wednesday night and reschedule our visit with the good padre for a later date.

In mid October our high school graduating class had its 40th reunion. Carroll Ann and I attended the Saturday night gathering, and as usual it was a fun evening. I was leaving for Saltillo the next afternoon. We were sitting in my classmate's den eating a buffet style dinner when another former classmate and his wife walked into the room and sat across from us on the fireplace stoop. I hadn't seen Andy in perhaps 20 years. We struck up a conversation and over a period of time, when asked what I had been doing recently, I mentioned Mexico and Saltillo. They both simultaneously asked, "You must know Padre Quinn?" "No," I responded, "but I can see there is an urgency for me to meet him." The next morning I called Mike and told him of the third incident of "you must know Padre Quinn" and that we needed to stay in Saltillo and keep our Thursday date with the priest.

We finished up our business and Thursday morning we headed for the downtown parish of Our Lady of Guadalupe. Padre Quinn was 67 years old and had been in Saltillo for 27 years. He looked more than his age. He was a quiet man and volunteered nothing about himself. We had gone suspecting that we were being led to help him financially with his food ministry. I asked him what his main food supplies were and he answered corn meal and beans. He distributed 50 tons of corn meal in 2½ pound bags per month. Later I would understand that the Catholics in Mississippi were sending him a significant amount of money each year in support of his work with the poor. At that point,

I knew that our meeting the padre had nothing to do with financial help. He was well supported by the good people in Mississippi, and their money was well spent.

After talking a while we asked him if he would take us around and show us some of the areas he worked in. He agreed and we rode in a large white van. Father sat in the front next to the driver, and I sat directly behind him and leaned forward to talk with him. He first took us to see a church that was being rehabilitated. He told us that he had build more than 35 churches over the past 27 years. He then took us to the local barrio of Monterrey and drove us through an area that was totally foreign to anything either one of us had ever seen. There were several square miles of 12' x 12' scrap wood shacks sitting on barren land and not a tree to be found. There was no electricity and therefore no lighting. The priest related that the people's lives began and ended with the rising and setting of the sun, one of the reasons the population was out of control. Nothing else to do once the sun goes down. No water or bathroom facilities. An open 55-gallon drum sat in front of each shack, and once or twice per week a city owned tanker came by and filled the drums with water of unknown quality. Sprinkled in amongst the wood shacks were a few concrete block one room structures, a little larger, but still one room for a family. The priest used donations from the states to buy the blocks, rebar, sand and cement. The locals built their own homes in their spare time. Often neighbors would help each other. Surprisingly this was not an area of homeless people that we as Americans had assumed. These were simply the homes of the working poor. A Mexican laborer might make $2 American per day, with no benefits, unless he worked for a maquiladora (a foreign owned industry that manufactured in Mexico but exported all its products). The maquilas hired locals and those fortunate enough to land jobs could study English and better their family's lot. Without the foreign work opportunities, a poor and uneducated Mexican was destined to live and die in the barrios.

Padre Quinn took us to visit a group of cloistered nuns who were excited to receive him and his American guests. Everyone who came up to the priest kissed his ring. It was truly an experience to see the love these people had for him.

We spent about five hours with him, then we returned to his church and he gave us a tour of the facilities. I can only describe it as looking like a complex of additions. Over the years he had added dormitory style living quarters. Each summer the families in Mississippi sent groups of chaperoned teenagers to stay with Padre Quinn and work in the field with the poor Mexicans. It was a toss up as to who benefited whom. As usual God's way is always a win-win. He had added doctors' and dentists' offices on the premises and each day a volunteer manned them.

As we road through the barrio I seemed to be given the right questions to ask him. He had come to America from Ireland 30 some years ago and had been assigned a four-year tour of duty in Mexico. He did not like it and was preparing to leave when his time was up. A year before he was to leave he was in a terrible automobile accident that left him relegated to recovery in a wheel chair for over 12 months. He learned during that year that God wanted him to stay in Mexico and he never left.

We left Saltillo that Thursday evening with much to contemplate. We talked about what we had seen during the nine-hour trip home. We couldn't believe the things we had seen and the way the people obviously adored this priest, and his reciprocal love for them. As we continued to muse over our experience and tried to relate it to others, we realized that we had come back with no pictures. Words could not describe what we had seen. Mike was even more in awe than I was. I was later to learn that my single partner changed his life insurance to make Padre Quinn his sole beneficiary. We knew the next time we returned to Saltillo we would be armed with still and video cameras. The next trip would not be until mid December.

We again called the padre and told him we would like to see him in December and that we would like to get pictures to show Americans the work he was doing. He agreed to meet with us and to escort us around the barrios again. We took several rolls of film and had more conversation with the priest. As we took pictures I realized that the children were not rag-a-muffins that you would expect to see in homeless surroundings. It was then that I realized this was not a community of homeless people but rather the working poor. The people were reasonably well dressed. They loved having their pictures taken, and though I could not verbally communicate with them we all seemed to enjoy the encounter. As we left Mike made the comment to me, "the priest does not look well."

We departed Mexico around December 20. Christmas is the really big Mexican holiday and the country literally shuts down until after New Year's Day. During this time there are very intense family gatherings and religious celebrations.

Around January 10, I returned from a three-day business trip to Chicago. My wife picked me up at the airport and about half way home she said, "we got a call from Saltillo today and Padre Quinn died of a heart attack last night." I was stunned. The pit of my stomach sank. How could this be, I asked myself in silence. My wife knew how much I had thought of this man and how I had referred to him as the closest thing to a saint I had ever been around. We finished the ride home in silence.

I spent that weekend in solemn contemplation. What was this all about? First I knew that I had been led to meet this man with some degree of urgency. The fact that three different people had asked me if I knew Padre Quinn, the meetings and the pictures were all evidence that I was supposed to meet this holy man. We were probably the last Americans to visit and talk with the priest, given the intensity of the Christmas celebration that went on through early January. I realized that he never volunteered any information, but that I had learned a lot about his life, the food he distributed, the clothing and medical care he provided, sometimes smuggling medicine across the border, the churches he had helped build, the material he provided for homes, the masses he had said, the confession he had heard. The priest had baptized and buried all of these people for 27 years, and now, when they still needed him, he was suddenly gone.

We had been privileged to see and hear all about this saintly man and yet now he was dead. All weekend I contemplated what had happened, and, finally, I understood the lesson for myself. My concept of what God should or shouldn't do has no bearing on what He does. I understood that each of our souls and God know what our missions are when we come to this earth, our missions being to execute God's Will for us as He allows them to occur. When those missions are completed God brings our soul home to Himself. Sometimes those missions involve leaving humans behind with uncertainty as to what has happened and why. Sometimes a person will suffer a long and painful death and we wonder why. That person might have agreed to endure a lengthy illness in dignity, with courage, simply to affect some seemingly insignificant bystander. It might be a janitor cleaning the floors outside her hospital room every night. Hearing her pray aloud to God in thanks for all the blessings she and her family have received could have quite an impact on this unbelieving, or faltering, janitor, knowing full well the people in this ward are terminally ill with cancer. What impact would that kind of faith have on this seemingly insignificant bystander?

Perhaps a nurse, struggling with her faith, watches one of her patents suffer and die, witnessing the patent's acceptance of going home to God. That's what I learned that weekend. How could God take someone who was playing such an important role in the daily lives of literally thousands of poor Mexicans? I realized that it was not for me to question. It had been an agreement between the good padre's soul and God.

They buried him in the back of the church in an above ground vault. Two or three months later we were again in Satillo and we visited the church. I remember sitting there praying and then walking outside. I went back inside and touched the vault and said goodbye to a seemingly old friend. It was an emotional moment for me. I knew that God had allowed me to meet a saint.

When he died there were several pages in the Mississippi newspaper about his life. What was truly amazing was that though I had met this man only twice, once for five hours, and once for two hours, he was not talkative and

I had to ask questions to get any information, I already knew everything that was in the four-page newspaper article. I'm not sure to this day exactly why we were led to meet him. I think it was to impact my partner. He began going to church regularly and reading a Bible that I left on his table. It also gave us insight into what was going to with the poor people of Mexico.

Most importantly I think that it was for me to learn the lesson of "why bad things happen to good people." That often used phrase is of human origin. We believe, because we don't understand the full scope of God's plan, that dying or suffering is a bad thing. I began to understand that God takes us, not when we are ready, but when He is ready. Those left behind grieve, but the returning soul is in glory with God.

As the years have passed I have come to believe this story is one for the bereaved. I unintentionally told this story to a classmate who had lost his wife to cancer about three to four weeks earlier. We had lunch together and I was sort of struggling for conversation, trying to keep it going and not wanting to only talk about business given that he had just lost his wife. Yet I had difficulty bringing up a subject that might help him or relate to his grief.

As lunch went on we talked about business and Mexico and our grandchildren. He then asked me if I thought it was still a business or a mission. I told him we were going to Mexico the following week to check out what kind of feeling I would get about moving there for something other than work. I told him we would revisit some of the ministries we had been working with for the past five years.

He then asked me to tell him about some of our ministry work in Mexico. I began to tell him the story of how I was led to meet Padre Quinn. How I met three different people in a short period of time and how they asked if I knew the priest. How we had gone down there and met him and went back the second time for pictures and how we left in late December with the movie and still pictures. How I had gone on a business trip in early January and returned to find that Mexico had called, and Padre Quinn had suddenly died of a heart attack.

I started to tell him how I had struggled that weekend to understand how someone doing such wonderful work, could be suddenly taken by God. As I began this part of the conversation I knew without planning where my story was going. I was being led to share with him my feelings about how bad things happen to good people, how even though we think someone is doing really good things, when their mission(s) or purpose(s) in life is over, God brings them home. Our idea of what is important in life is not necessarily what God thinks is important. How people touch others in their dying, and in their actual death. How they, and those around them suffering in dignity, impact peripheral persons around the suffering family. It is God's way of teaching people, by using people. My friend started to tear up.

Nickey Ho had told me, "you will see it in their eyes" when a healing has begun to take place. I'm not sure that he knew it, but his emotional healing had begun.

I can never cease to marvel at how and why God uses me to be his instrument in these episodes. I had not a clue where the conversation was going until I was into the part about Padre Quinn dying. The Holy Spirit was with me.

Story # 8
We Don't Have Any Poor

In 1982 we had been in business for 10 years, and by most cultural guidelines were financially successful. I was 42 years old and within our small circle of friends we were affectionately known as "the newly rich." Rich was an over statement, but for the first time in our lives we were not living from paycheck to paycheck. I had begun developing my hip pocket theology and I knew that I was subservient to God. I began to have a feeling inside of me that something was missing. I could not identify it, but I knew that it was related to my business success, and the feeling was that I should be giving something back. It would persist through 1982 and into the following year.

My wife, my daughter and I had moved into a condo in the county and we were attending a Catholic Church nearby. I had become active in my college alma mater, a Catholic college, but the participation did not satiate the distant calling I was feeling.

One Sunday at Mass the priest gave his homily on "feeding the hungry and clothing the naked." I knew in that moment that he was talking to me. The proverbial light went on in my head and I knew that feeding the hungry was what God was calling me to do. I was excited beyond myself. I could hardly wait for the next morning. I waited until 8:05 that Monday morning and

I called the rectory. As God would have it the priest, who was the pastor who gave the homily, answered the telephone. I told him I had heard his message and that I knew God had been calling me to feed the hungry and then I asked how I could get started. In a very detached voice he responded with "we don't have any poor people in our parish." I was speechless. I had heard this man deliver the message to me the previous morning in church. Something inside me said, "let it go" and I politely ended the conversation without verbalizing the resistance I was feeling. When I hung up the telephone I actually questioned whether I had heard what I thought I heard. Did I dream this? What did he mean by "We don't have any poor people in our parish?" Then I became angry. I had heard about feeding the poor all of my life. In the parochial elementary school I attended, each week we were asked to give our pennies to the St. Vincent DePaul Society that spends its resources to help the poor.

I went to the telephone directory and called another Catholic church. The priest on the other end of the phone said "We don't have any poor people in our parish." I called a second number and got the same words "We don't have any poor people in our parish." The third call yielded exactly the same words. I put down the telephone in disbelief. All of my life I had heard of the many poor people in the world. Now there were no poor to be found. I knew I had to reflect on what was happening. There was a message here but I was not getting it. Two weeks later some old friends were at our home for dinner when I related this strange story to them. One of them said, "Nathan you should call Monsignor Clunan. He is very much involved with the poor." The next day I did call him. The good monsignor chuckled and said yes, indeed he had more poor people than he could deal with, and he invited me to come and talk with him.

That was the beginning of a friendship that continued on until he retired and later passed away. When I had thought of feeding the poor I conceived the thought of helping the "newly poor." Those people who had worked all their lives and through no fault of their own had lost their jobs. The monsignor had other ideas, and as I sent him money each month, he told me he was using it for the inner city poor. This wasn't what I wanted and I was prepared to confront him with my thoughts and desires for the use of my money when God intervened with a thought that I knew I must abide. The thought was "you provide the financial means. Let the priest determine where it is to be used." Thus began my first encounter with the concept of being part of the Body of Christ. It was my first experience with not controlling how my money would be used. It would be only the initial stage of a lesson I needed to learn, that would eventually free me of one of my worldly gods.

As time elapsed I was amazed that God would contact me so directly, and the use of money for good in a spiritual sense was foreign to everything I had ever heard. All of my early training talked about giving everything away in order to follow Christ. Yet as time went by I would learn that for all of the people God calls to hands-on ministry, someone else has to supply the money that allows all of those good things to happen. I began to question whether this was a true calling. This was the beginning of my bartering with God. It would be several years later that I would read Genesis 18, where Abraham barters with God for the sparing of Sodom. I would go for a walk and I would tell God that I was going to increase the stipend to the monsignor. If this was truly what He wanted He would have to provide the means for me to sustain this new level of giving. He never failed me.

In the following 18 months I continued to increase the giving with the same admonition to God. In that period, on at least a dozen occasions God revealed His answer to me in the same repetitious manner, allowing me to know that it was not coincidental. I would write the checks for our monthly bills and I would always write the check to the monsignor last. When finished I would then balance our checkbook. On at least a dozen occasions I found a deposit that had not been recorded, or an addition or subtraction error almost identical to the amount of the check for the charity. At the end of the check writing it was as if the donation check never happened. It was God's way of letting me know that he would provide the means.

There was one specific incident that remains with me until this day. Our company had bid on a very large government contract and when the sealed bids were opened we were number 24 in the order of competitive pricing, hardly a spot for optimism. Again on a lengthy walk I spoke to God and promised Him that if we were awarded this contract I would donate 25 percent of our profits from that work to the poor. As I reflect back on that time I don't recall thinking the prayer was one of desperation, but of reality, in spite of our 24th price ranking.

A couple of weeks later I received a call from our office saying they had just received a communication from the government announcing that a week earlier they had faxed the bidders an "extension of price" agreement that was to be signed and returned to the government. One of our junior employees had picked up the document and alerted our president of the request, and we had properly responded. Apparently 12 of the 23 in front of us had failed to respond to the request and had been disqualified. We were now 11th on the list. Eighteen months later the 10 companies in front of us were disqualified for technical deficiencies, and our company was awarded the single largest five-year contract in its history. Needless to say, each month I computed the profit from the job and dutifully sent the check to the monsignor. Jesus says, "if you have faith of a mustard seed you can move mountains." (Luke 17,6).

God gave me a small taste of His awesome power when we are in concert with His Will. Eighteen years later I unexpectedly attended a St. Vincent DePaul Society meeting in a nearby parish. There were about 12 persons there. As the meeting went on it became obvious that most of us were first time attendees. There were a number of questions about how the society discovered the needy and how they dealt with the financial burdens. Finally someone asked the leaders a question. "Father, it sounds like you are responding to poor people all across the city. Do you ever get any calls from poor people in our parish?" The leaders looked at each other and then at the priest. They all indicated no with the shaking of their heads. The priest then said "We don't have any poor people in our parish." I would have fallen out of my chair had it not been for the table I could lean on. After all these years the words I had heard, and never quite let go of, had been repeated, verbatim.

I went home that night knowing that God had given me the privilege of another lesson. I dwelt on it for several days. I am not here to criticize the priests. The simple fact is that we humans have our own agendas. We are all called to serve God in our own ways. Some priests and ministers are tuned to helping drug addicts, or saving marriages, or helping children. It is truly an illustration of the Body of Christ. Each of us has his cross to bear, his calling from God, his way to follow Christ. Each of us must seek the Will of the Father for himself, for others are, or should be, seeking it for themselves. The words confirmed that I needed to pursue my calling to feed the hungry with even more passion, for not everyone is tuned into the fact that an empty stomach can hear nothing good, much less the Word of God.

Story # 9
Wisdom Without Bounds

In the early winter of 1999 I had lunch with a minister friend of mine. We often got together to discuss what God was doing in our lives. On this particular day we had planned to meet at a very popular restaurant near his church. When we arrived we found it was too busy to accommodate us. He then suggested a place where he often ate. They had a very good catfish buffet lunch and it was never very crowded.

We ate and talked at a leisurely pace for a long while. Out of the corner of my eyes I could see patrons coming and going as we lingered around. At some point, and for some unknown reason, I began to tell him my story and encounter with my pornography addiction. As I spoke to him, with no agenda on my part, I noticed a tear running down his cheek and I immediately knew that we had been led to this off beat restaurant with God's Plan in mind. All he said was "I need to see him." At that moment I knew that God was asking me to take this minister, who could not afford the trip on his own, to Sarasota. I told him I would take him whenever he was ready.

In late January 2000 we flew to Sarasota. We arrived and he had his first session with Richard on Tuesday. I saw Richard myself on a couple of days, but mostly the trip was for my friend. During the day between sessions we drove around talking about God and looking at the sights. I remember after his first session we went walking around the pier area near downtown Sarasota. We were almost back to our car when I began to feel extremely nauseated and light headed. I actually felt like I would have trouble making it back to the car. Suddenly I realized what was happening. It had been about an hour since his session with Richard and he was dissipating some of this pent up negative energy and I, as usual, was sponging it up. I immediately went through my clearing prayer asking God to take any negative energy I was absorbing and give it back to the universe. Within five minutes the symptoms disappeared. As we were driving out of the pier area my friend mentioned that he felt like a great load had been lifted from his shoulders. I commented jokingly "yea, and I can feel it." Once again God had prepared me to deal with negative energy absorbed during a psychological healing.

The week passed on. We talked all day and into the night about God and how he was working with us, and the miracle of our minds. How we never know from whence and where God will show up to give us what we need most. On one occasion he told me a most fascinating story of how, as a young married man struggling to finish seminary, he had reached a point where it looked impossible that he would be able to financially manage full time school and paying his bills. He mentioned that one night he had prayed for "wisdom without bounds" and went on to tell a fascinating story of how God gave him that wisdom and his schooling and finances were taken care of. I fell in love with the story and I thought about it often during the next few days.

In the evenings we would find a reasonably nice restaurant and I would have a couple of Scotch and sodas and he a couple of beers. By 10:00 we were in our rooms and I easily drifted off to sleep. On Friday night, following the same ritual, I lay in bed and earnestly prayed to God for wisdom without bounds. I rolled over and expected to drift off to sleep. Yet sleep did not come, and after an hour or so I rolled onto my back and wondered what was going on. At that moment my mind was filled with the dominating thought, "Stop drinking for a year." I knew immediately what the thought meant. Stop drinking alcohol for a year. My first reaction was one of chuckle and disbelief. I spoke half aloud, with the intent of humor. "Come on now. Ask for my leg or my arm, but don't ask me to give up the couple of drinks each evening that I like so much." Yet the thought persisted. My response was, "I need time to think about this." Then I rolled over and drifted off to sleep.

The next morning I joined my friend for breakfast and jokingly told him his story of wisdom without bounds had gotten me in way over my head. Then I related the previous night's experience. He asked, "What are you going to do?" I responded that I didn't know. It was a big decision that I could not make easily. I knew enough to know that if I made the commitment to God I would keep it. My relationship with God is an honest one, to my conscious knowledge. By lunch I had begun to think of all the sanctimonious rhetoric I had spouted during the past few years. I told myself that I "could talk the talk," but could I "walk the walk?" It was a defining moment in my thought process. That Saturday evening I had a glass of tea with dinner. That was the beginning of 12 months of sobriety and unusual pain and experiences that would set my life back on course.

It was now the first part of February and we were very much still struggling with our Mexico venture. It had been six months since our last major project had concluded. Yet the expenses related to our sales effort in Mexico continued. About two weeks into the non-drinking mode I began to have a knot in my stomach almost every afternoon and the only release I would get would be exercising on my treadmill. When it persisted I thought it might be withdrawal pains from habitual drinking, but after six weeks I knew that was not the case. I had never had more than a couple of drinks an evening. The pains grew more intense as did the need to deal with Mexico. One day as I was headed home from my office my stomach distention became almost unbearable. As I drove into my driveway I said aloud in desperation, "God tell me what to do about Mexico. I have no idea what to do. Jesus I give this to you. Help me." I proceeded into my home and changed into my exercise clothing, knowing the treadmill would bring me relief. It is important to note that at that point, almost two months into the non-drinking and in spite of the pain, I was never seriously tempted to drink.

Within five minutes on the treadmill and still praying to God for an answer, it came. The thought that filled my mind was "Go to Mexico. Go for longer than the week you normally go. Do not make many planned business meetings. Leave time open. Revisit the three ministries you have been dealing with these past five years. And take your wife with you." By the end of 30 minutes the pain was gone, but not the message. At this point I believed that God was sending us to Mexico to make plans for moving there. I had come to believe that if Mexico was going to happen for our company my presence would be the catalyst.

Though always willing to support my endeavors, my wife was not anxious to spend 10 days in Mexico. We would stay with our Mexican friends and it would be very comfortable. They were always the most hospitable and giving people I have ever met. They gave of themselves with ease and sincere love.

The first couple of days we made business calls and I witnessed my two employees "at work." I knew in those two meetings they would not successfully sell engineering services. On an open day, my friend and host suggested that we revisit some of the regulatory offices we had met with over the past several years. This would happen on three different days. Each office closed the door on our potential for work. I began to visualize the events as a large circle that was slowly closing on itself. Doors closing say as much as, or more than, doors opening.

On the second day I had dinner with the head of one of the ministries I had been working with for more than three years. I paid close attention to everything that happened and was spoken, looking for some sign that was calling us to Mexico. The evening brought nothing new.

At the end of the first week we arranged to spend time with the second ministry and went into the countryside with Padre Quinn's replacement, Father Miguel, to a small village miles into the Monterrey desert. While wonderfully adventurous, the day brought nothing from the priest that would justify the instructions to revisit the ministries.

By now the circle of opportunity in Mexico had closed to the point that I could see this was not a visit of beginning, but rather a visit of ending. On one of the final days I met with a priest who was head of small retreat house run by the Brothers of St. John, a French-based order with the primary purpose of conducting retreats for the people. The priest was very pleasant. I had not met him personally, but at the urging of my hostess, who was very active with the retreat home, we had sent him a monthly stipend for the past couple of years. We sat across from one another in a stark little mission room, and I began telling him my story of how I had come to Mexico to clean the water to make money to help feed the poor. I then mentioned Padre Quinn. When I did the priest literally picked up my conversation and began to expound about the saintly priest, whom he had never met but who represented all that he wanted to do for the poor people that surrounded him. I sat in astonishment. I knew the answer to "revisit the three ministries" was here with this priest. That evening we talked for about two hours. After the first 10 minutes I mostly listened to the priest.

The day before we were to leave I revisited the priest and the conversation picked up where we left off. He wanted desperately to help the poor, yet every time he made plans to expand his ministry his resources would evaporate. Finally, after two more hours, my wife and friends were knocking on the door and wanting to leave. In the last couple of minutes of our four-hour visit all that needed to be said was said. I leaned forward in my chair and I spoke to the priest. "Five years ago I came to Mexico with a most noble idea to clean the water and to make money to feed the poor. And as noble as that idea was, it simply did not happen. So now I will leave here and perhaps I will never return." He looked across the table at me and he said, "If it is God's Will, He will bless it." At that moment I knew that I had come two thousand miles to look into a mirror and see that I was not the only one who often erred in noble ideas. The priest and I warmly shook hands, knowing that we had experienced God in each other. Later that evening, as I lay in bed at our friend's home, I knew that Mexico was over for me. "If it is God's Will He will bless it."

When we returned home I wrote priest the following letter.

MAY 6, 2000

Father Tarcisius

Congregation San Juan

Dear Fr. Tarcisius;

I have been planning to write this note to you since we returned from our trip to Mexico. I have thought about you often. Today is a rainy Saturday morning so I am catching up on tasks that need doing.

I feel that my 10 day trip to Mexico answered all of my questions. Everything I was told to do yielded conclusive results. Meeting and exchanging our stories was probably the most important part of that process. After I left you Monday night, and we got back to Leon & Elvira's home, and I was lying in bed the thoughts below came to me and I wrote them down. As I am writing this letter it seems right to share them with you.

In the last couple of minutes of our Monday night meeting all that needed to be said, was said. It was time for me to leave. I offered that I would be around for two more days and that you could call me if you wanted to talk further. You said, "no, that all of this is in God's hands, and I will not be calling you."

As we were about to part I said. "Father, five years ago I had this very noble idea about coming down to Mexico and cleaning the water and making enough money to help people like yourself, help the poor. So far, as noble as the idea was, it has not happened." You responded, "if something is God's Will He will bless it." For all of the hours that we spoke and listened to each other these few words summed up the entire encounter. I had traveled 2000 miles to tell my story to a man and to listen to his story. As I left you I realized that each of us had been looking into a mirror. Both of us had noble ideas of helping the poor but God had not blessed our quest, at least not in the fashion we had envisioned. I realized, as I left you, that perhaps my encounter with you was my last direct involvement with Mexico. I had that same feeling when we left Leon's home on Wednesday morning. It was a feeling of closure, sadness and farewell.

These few thoughts really do say it all. Since I have returned home I feel at peace, and I know that at this time, I am not supposed to be in Mexico. The constant anxiety of "what does God want of me" has left and I am at peace with myself. I hope our encounter was also of benefit to you.

I find these experiences with God to be awesome and humbling. Why He continues to bless me I cannot say. I am always grateful that He is using me. When I first started studying Paul's Epistles I thought "this guy is always bragging about his relationship with God." It sort of turned me off. However, I now realize that sharing your God experiences with others and acknowledging that it is only through Him these things happen, we are giving honor and glory to His name.

I hope my "feeling of closure and finality" was limited to the business aspect of Mexico and that I will see all of my friends (both new and old) for many years in the future. If this turns out to be my last visit to Mexico, then I am at peace with that reality. I have nothing but pleasant thoughts and feelings about my experiences in the last five years, and all of the fantastic people I have met in Mexico.

Part of what I learned was that at this time there is not enough environmental work in Mexico to support our business. However, the man who has worked with me for over 28 years has elected to stay in Saltillo. I believe there is enough work to support a one, or two, man operation. He has married a young Mexican woman and at this point it would seem that perhaps our coming to Mexico was mainly to get him away from the States and into an environment where he could get his life together. He could use all of the prayers you and your Brothers can offer in his name. (Leon and Elvira know him well.)

The mail service between here and Mexico is slow at best. I hope you get this note and I pray it finds you too at peace with yourself and God. You and your mission are in my prayers. If you get the urge to write, I will be happy to hear from you. I will always remember how God brought two strangers together to share their common vision about helping the poor, and yet bowing to His Will.

Love in Christ,

Nathan Pera

PS; since starting to write this three weeks ago I can give you an update. For the first time in almost five years I am without pain or anxiety over what I should be doing. Perhaps this is God's way of blessing me for my following Him long enough to get my young friend to Mexico. I still think the last few minutes together and your words "If something is God's Will, He will bless it," still stand out as the "trip's message."

(End of letter)

———————————

The venture in Mexico was over for me. I knew that I needed to close out the financial support we had been pumping into Mexico for the past three years. My partner, living in Mexico with his new Mexican wife, would have to make a decision to either return to the States or stay in Mexico as a self-sufficient profit center. Not surprisingly he choose to stay in Mexico. And so, after five years and a lot of wonderful adventures, he would be the only one to realize his dream. At the beginning in 1995 he stated his goal for the business venture was to experience the Mexican culture. He had certainly accomplished that goal. I am proud that he stayed and carried on the dream we started.

Once we terminated the Mexican venture my stomach discomfort disappeared. I realized that drinking had masked my pain. The pain I would have felt if I were not drinking would have led me to understand that something in my life was off center. Once I had stopped using the masking agent (alcohol) I was forced to address the source of my pain and the reason I was off center. It was time to let go of Mexico.

One day at lunch with a new friend, who happened to be another priest, I told him of my praying for wisdom without bounds and the resulting Mexico experience. When I finished he stopped eating, looked up at me and said simply, "you were obedient." In all the months of abstaining from alcohol I had never looked at it from the perspective of obedience. Yet I knew he was right. I had taken on the challenge because I knew that God would reveal Himself to me in an unusual way if I kept my promise. I knew that my prayer for wisdom would be answered, and I wouldn't miss His message of wisdom for the world. A purist may say my motivation was not of the highest order, and I would agree. I have found that God works with each of us with what He finds available in us. I had come to know God as a friend who loves one-on-one exchanges with me, and if I heeded His request or command, I would find it a mutually rewarding adventure. After all, what is life if it is not a spiritual adventure?

So the 12-month period of sobriety ended in February of 2001, and since that time God has given me insights far beyond my mental capacities. But those are stories still unfolding and for another time. Specifically I would mention *Prostate & Cancer, I've Been Where You are Going.* Another book now in editing.

CHAPTER 13
EPILOGUE

As I have finished the stories describing this phase of my spiritual journey, I feel compelled to give further explanations, yet it comes to me there is nothing more to say for now. This is my story, no one else's. I cannot explain to anyone how my story relates to his or her journey. That is for readers to conclude for themselves. As for me, what comes next is unknown. That is what my life's journey is about, stepping forward with an acceptance that whatever God has in mind for me He will unfold in His own time, and when it is best for me and for those whom He will lead me to encounter.

In the Gospels, Jesus commands that the little children be allowed to come to him, for the kingdom of heaven is of such as these (Matthew 19:14). Without appearing self-righteous I feel my theology allows me, like a child, to look into everything that is and see the Creator who made it. I try, but rarely succeed, to share my blessings with love as Jesus commands. I live in a world where everything is possible if I simply let the Spirit of God work through me (John 14:11-14). It dawns on me that since my awakening I have become more childlike in my belief in God's presence in every moment of my life. I am eternally thankful and unworthy of that blessing.

The Bible is the most metaphysical book I have ever read. For me the words convey the Word of God to man through His Son, Jesus Christ. For me the Bible continues to be the gateway to the reality of the spiritual world.

If I could leave the reader with one thought it would be to follow your own heart. I did not reveal my story so that you could emulate it, I wrote it in hopes that it will give you courage to pursue your own truth through a direct encounter with God who dwells within you. Share your experiences with all who will listen or read. Seek out God's will for you.

CONTACT THE AUTHOR
EMAIL

Since my purpose in publishing this book is helping other people of any religion, or no religion, who may be struggling with the issues I have described, I invite you, the reader, to contact me if you feel the need to discuss details of these issues that the book has not covered. I will reply as best I can to any sincere request for help. Please note, however, that I do not invite, nor will I respond to, correspondence from those who wish to argue theology or to challenge the authenticity of my personal experiences.

Nathan Pera, Sr.

Nathan2924@aol.com

ABOUT THE AUTHOR

Nathan A. Pera, III is Chairman and CEO of three environmental engineering and testing firms he founded, beginning in 1972. He is active in inter-denominational youth ministries in Memphis where he was born and raised. A chemist and engineer by education and training, Nathan finds time to write between managing his businesses and his community projects.

A talented athlete, a good, but not great student, he was twenty-one years of age and a senior at Christian Brothers University before he discovered his capacity to succeed in school and later in what ever he was led to do.

His writing style, he says, "just showed up one day. I sat down one day to tell my story hoping just one person might benefit from reading it. For some reason I haven't stopped writing."

The author has two more books in the editing stage *(Prostate & Cancer, I've Been Where You are Going,* and *Contemplating the Presence of God)* due for release later this year. If they are as compelling and graphic as this one they will be well received.

Nathan lives in Memphis with his high school sweetheart and wife of more than 40 years. "You can reclaim your life."

Printed in the United States
24321LVS00001B/49-111

9 781418 495831